D1553404

The Case for Taking the Date out of Rape

The Case for Taking the
Date out of Rape

AILEEN McCOLGAN

An Imprint of HarperCollins*Publishers*

Pandora
An Imprint of HarperCollinsPublishers
77-85 Fulham Palace Road,
Hammersmith, London W6 8JB

Published by Pandora 1996
1 3 5 7 9 10 8 6 4 2

A catalogue record for this book
is available from the British Library

ISBN 0 04 440977 X

Printed and bound in Great Britain by
Caledonian International Book Manufacturing Ltd, Glasgow

To Robbie

Contents

Acknowledgements ix

PART ONE: THE BACKGROUND

1   Date Rape in Context 3
2   A Brief History of Rape 12

PART TWO: THE CASE

3   The Birth of Date Rape 31
4   The Forms of Denial in the Media 42
5   The Forms of Denial in Society 54
6   The Forms of Denial in the Legal System 67

PART THREE: CONCLUSION

7   The Reality of Rape 93

References 109

Acknowledgements

Thanks are due to Robbie for pressurizing me into writing this, to Ken Oliphant for his painstaking commentary on earlier versions and to Matt Fox, Guy Jones and Kristina Stern as well as to Sara Dunn at Pandora for her excellent editing.

PART I

The Background

1

Date Rape in Context

For decades, women in many countries across the world have struggled to improve the way in which rape is dealt with by the police, the courts and society at large. They have also struggled against the myths which persist about those who complain of rape; women really want it; women say 'no' when they mean 'yes'; women get what they deserve, and so on.

Some victories have been won. Here in the United Kingdom, for example, police practice has been improved and a number of legal changes have been made. Women are less likely to be bullied and abused when they report rape to the police. They are likely to be interviewed in the relatively comfortable surroundings of a rape suite; and to have their medical examination carried out, if they wish, by a female doctor. Their names will be kept secret by the press (at least as soon as a man is charged with rape), and their court appearances should be much less harrowing than they would have been twenty years ago – not least because the trial should be more concerned with the defendant's guilt than with the number of men the woman has slept with. Finally, since 1995, judges are no longer required to warn juries that women are inclined to lie about allegations of rape.

That is, at least, the theory. In practice, not every police station has rape suite facilities, and women who report rape ('complainants') may be questioned in a draughty interview room and examined in the local casualty department after a lengthy wait. Even in London, the woman who accused Craig Charles of rape (he was subsequently acquitted) had to wait seven hours before a female doctor could be found to examine her – small wonder that by then she just wanted to go home to sleep.

Many police officers are still very suspicious of women who complain of rape. There is still a widespread belief that women often lie about rape. The result of this is that large numbers of rape reports are written-off by the police. And for all the changes in the law, women's ordeals in court are every bit as bad as they ever were – and the press seem to be even more interested now than they used to be. Irrelevant details of women's sex lives are plastered over the front pages of tabloid newspapers (and mentioned, albeit in smaller print, by the 'quality' press). The newspapers may be prevented from publishing complainants' names, addresses and identifying photographs (unless the judge or the woman herself decide otherwise). But there is nothing to stop them from publishing the sorts of details which would make a woman identifiable to those who know her – and these are the people from whom she may most want to keep her 'private' life private.

Even if a woman is one of the 10 per cent of complainants who manages to get her case as far as the criminal courts, the chances are that her attacker will be acquitted – in 1993, less than one in ten reported rape cases resulted in a conviction. She will have spent days being interviewed by the police; undergone a distressing medical examination; and put her life on hold for the one to two years it takes

for the case to come to court: she will have been through what is
generally an extremely humiliating cross-examination by the man's
lawyer, as well as having to relive the details of the attack for the
benefit of the jury. The man's lawyer will have questioned her about
her sexual habits, past boyfriends, use of contraception and any
history of abortion, depression, and so on. He or she will have done
their damnedest to paint her as a 'slag'. All of this will have been
reported with relish in the press. Despite all this, there is now a
common school of thought which contends that, by way of icing
on the cake, her attacker will usually be acquitted.

Men, rather than women, are now the victims of rape. Men
are being victimized by a flood of false allegations of rape; by the
redefinition as rape of bad sex, of drunken sex, of any sex which is
less than orgasmic and stone-cold sober. Innocent men, we are told,
are suffering. And women are to blame.

This new victimhood has been crystallized by the term 'date
rape', and debated around a handful of high-profile cases. When the
men concerned are acquitted, as they almost invariably have been,
they are idolized by the press, re-cast as the heroic victims of
vindictive and untruthful trollops.

Austen Donnellan had, by his own admission, had sex with
a falling-down-drunk woman who had consistently rejected his
advances when sober. When he was acquitted, almost every
newspaper in the land proclaimed him the innocent victim of lunatic
feminism. According to the *Independent* Craig Charles was greeted
as a returning hero after he was acquitted of (gang) raping his ex-
girlfriend in March 1995. 'Charles was recognized by fans at roughly
100 yard intervals. All of them seemed to be chuffed for Craig. A taxi
driver shouted "Craig! Nice one!" A courier ... "Well done, Craig".'[1]

Even when men are convicted of rape, they may still find
themselves the objects of admiration (or, at worst, pity), rather than
scorn. When solicitor Angus Diggle was released after serving a year's

imprisonment for attempted rape, the Law Society (the solicitors' professional body) allowed him to resume work. (Pity, however, the man convicted of fare-dodging; he will not be allowed to practise.) An array of commentators pronounced him at the very least harshly treated, more often heinously wronged. According to Michael Vermeulen in the *Guardian* Diggle was 'a giggle', 'a pratt'.[2] According to Minnette Marrin in the *Sunday Telegraph*, he was 'a victim of our time'.[3] Mike Tyson, when he was released after serving three years for the rape of Desiree Washington in his Indianapolis hotel suite in 1991 – a conviction which the *Guardian* predicted would mean 'a certain end to his career'[4] – was given a hero's welcome.

Something odd is going on here. Men acquitted of rape are elevated into symbols of 'man oppressed by radical feminism'; MPs and newspapers call for complainants to be named when their alleged attackers are acquitted (as they generally are). Newspaper columns are filled with home-truths about girls who play with fire, and the dangers of mixing flirting and drink; politicians promise reviews of this law or that; and men and women journalists alike thunder about how feminism has got completely out of hand. Somehow, we are told, we have come to a point where all men are being portrayed as rapists, and all sex as rape.

But all the while, women are being raped, and men are getting away with it.

The very fact that women are complaining of date rape is, we are often told, symptomatic of a crisis in male-female relations. Gone are the days of sexual freedom, sex-as-fun. Gone are the days when men and women got drunk, fell into bed together, and accepted the consequences. Now, it seems, men and women get drunk, fall into bed together, and in the morning women cry 'rape'.

What can be done? The most common suggestion is that we have to distinguish more clearly between rape and sex. Rape, we are assured, is a wicked and dreadful crime, and those who are guilty of it

THE CASE FOR TAKING THE DATE OUT OF RAPE

should be severely punished. But, we are told, it is very important to draw a clear line between this and sex, whether that sex is unsatisfactory, mistaken, drunken or simply regretted in the morning. And it is this line, we are told, which is currently being blurred.

And how might you distinguish sex from rape? The legal distinction turns on the issue of consent – if a woman consents to penetration, that penetration qualifies as sex. If she does not consent then, providing the man knows that this is or may be the case, the penetration qualifies as rape. It seems to me that this is perfectly straightforward. Contrary to what is often suggested by the press, a man can't rape a woman by accident. A man can't rape a woman unless he *knows* that there is at least a chance that she isn't consenting to sex. If he makes a mistake, for some reason or another, and thinks that she is consenting when she is not, he is not guilty of rape. But, if he knows that there is a chance that the woman is not consenting (if, for example, she says 'no'), it is perfectly reasonable to demand that he should check. It doesn't take long, after all.

But this distinction is not enough to address the 'problem of date rape'. If you start from the premise that women lie about rape, the only way to define rape is to add a host of extra ingredients to the basic definition of sex without consent. You have to require that the woman was injured (to show that she *really* didn't want it). And you have to demand that the man was a total stranger to her (after all, she is more likely to consent to someone she knew than to a total stranger). You also have to demand that she has a good reputation – ideally she will be either very young or very old – a virgin, or at a push, a respectable married woman. Anyone else might be a 'slag'. And because even this is no guarantee of non-consent (there's a first time for everything), the man accused of rape has to be an evil monster.

The more qualifiers that are added, the closer this definition of rape gets to demanding that the raped woman be Little Red Riding

Hood, jumped upon by the evil wolf. Ludicrous as it sounds, it is only the rape of Little Red Riding Hood, which has been traditionally accepted as 'real' (or 'ideal') rape, both by the legal system and, more generally, by society.[5]

It is this tradition that underlies the recent controversies about date rape. Austen Donnellan's accuser was portrayed as a liar when he was acquitted of raping her – *The Times* claimed that the verdict meant the jury accepted that she 'made the allegation out of self-disgust that she could lose control and take to her bed a man she found sexually repellent'.[6] In fact, the verdict need not have meant anything of the sort. The woman was very drunk and, while she was convinced that she had been asleep when Donnellan had sex with her (this would have counted as rape), she couldn't *remember* what had happened. And, because she couldn't remember, the jury couldn't convict. Contrary to the line taken by *The Times* and by many other newspapers, Donnellan's acquittal *didn't* mean that she was lying.

Matthew Kydd's acquittal was secure as soon as the jury heard that his accuser had been voted 'slut of the year' at college (after all, how could a proclaimed slut be raped by anyone). Another man was acquitted despite it being accepted that the woman said no, and another despite his admission to the police that she did not consent to sex. Apart from the Donnellan case (which the defendant, rather than the woman, insisted be brought to trial – his college had attempted to deal with the matter internally and he wanted to clear his name), none of these cases sound like open and shut, clearly unfit-to-be-tried cases to me. But this is how they have been received by much of the press. Why? The bottom line is, because none of them fit the Little Red Riding Hood model. None of the women involved was purer than the driven snow. None of the men could be described as a monstrous sex beast. All of the people concerned in the cases knew each other. And in all of them, some level of consented-to sexual contact had taken place before the alleged rape.

THE CASE FOR TAKING THE DATE OUT OF RAPE

What really inspired the collective outrage of the press, politicians and so on was the belief that, *even if the men had behaved as the women claimed*, they still shouldn't have been on trial for rape. Because, whatever these men did, it couldn't be called rape. They hadn't jumped upon strangers in the dead of night. They hadn't viciously assaulted the women who accused them, they hadn't left their victims bleeding and bruised. They hadn't used weapons. And they hadn't even expressly threatened to harm the women if they didn't agree to sex. As one student said in the wake of Matthew Kydd's rape acquittal: 'This should never have come before a judge and jury. Rape is when a man with a knife threatens a woman with harm unless she does what he wants.'

It is precisely this notion that women have struggled against over the last twenty years. Because the fact is that most women who are raped are raped by men they know. Most of these men are not armed with knives, or with anything other than their fists, their penises and their superior strength. And a lot of these men don't even have to speak their threats out loud. In many cases, women know from bitter experience what the result of a struggle will be. In others, women are so shocked by a man's display of force (and this can simply be the force of penetrating her against her expressed wishes), that they are frozen into passivity. And sometimes, women are taken by surprise by men who just pin them down, or by men who ignore their 'no' and get on with it anyway.

It's these rapes which happen most frequently. It's these rapes which women are most likely to suffer. It's these rapes which the legal system has to deal with if it is to deal with the rapes which women actually *experience* (as opposed to those we tend to have nightmares about).

Women who have experienced the relative sexual freedom of modern times feel entitled to say yes to sex. But we also feel entitled to say no. This is why women are coming forward now to complain of being raped by men they know. It's not that these rapes have just started to happen – it is, rather, that women feel more entitled, and more able, to complain of them. And, just as this is beginning to happen, the backlash swings into action and the message is hammered home that this is date rape, and that date rape isn't rape.

In essence, the current reaction to date rape (the allegations of hysteria, of feminism gone mad and so on) is a conservative reaction to women's attempts to gain true sexual freedom – to be allowed to say no as well as yes. Sexual freedom isn't worth a damn if it doesn't include the freedom not to be forced into sex. It's all very well for men to claim that complaints about 'date rape' are anti-sexual freedom. But, after all, it suits men to define sexual freedom on their terms (i.e. as the freedom to fuck) because, unless they are attacked by other men, men are always free to refuse sex. All women are asking for is that we are allowed that same freedom.

To accept that date rape is rape isn't to say that all rapes are equally terrifying, that all rapists are equally evil. Obviously it is worse to be raped in circumstances where you fear death, and where you are left mutilated and half-dead, than it is simply to be overcome by force and left with no physical injuries. But it doesn't mean that you are not raped if you are not cut up as well. It doesn't mean that you are not raped if your rapist didn't hold a knife to your throat. And it certainly doesn't mean that you are not raped if the man who attacks you happens to be someone you have slept with before, someone who bought you dinner, someone you kissed.

Rape is rape is rape, like murder is murder is murder. Some rapes, some murders, are worse than others. But rape is rape. And murder is murder. Murder happens when a person deliberately kills someone. Rape happens when a man deliberately forces sex on an unwilling woman (or man). And this is all that 'rape' requires.

The rapes which are alleged in cases like Austen Donnellan's, even if the men are convicted, fall towards the bottom rather than the top of the scale of seriousness. Because in cases such as these penetration is achieved not by force or by threat but, rather, by surprise. But the fact that something is at the bottom of the scale doesn't mean that it isn't *on* the scale, and many rapes carried out by men known to their victims are every bit as violent as those carried out by strangers. In the United Kingdom more than three times as many rapes were reported in 1993 than in 1985. Only the same number of men were convicted, but women are at least complaining.[8] And it's this that freaks out the critics of date rape. Men are being accused of rape in circumstances where, until recently, women would have remained silent.

And it's this that threatens to blow open the subject of rape. Because the fact is (and it will become apparent in this book), rape is actually a very common event. Far from being restricted to the occasional fiend who goes prowling with a mask and a knife, rapists are ordinary men who live with women (often with the very women they attack), and have ordinary lives. Not *all* men are rapists. But many men are. Not *all* women have been raped. But many women have.

The arguments used by those who claim that date rape isn't rape are, in fact, the same arguments which have always been used to deny *most* rapes the status of a crime. They are the same arguments that have, in the past, been used to imprison or kill women for being raped. Women who complain of date rape today are disbelieved in the same way as most women who have complained of rape have always been disbelieved. To illustrate this point, I will start my case with a brief history of rape through the ages.

A Brief History of Rape

Two major themes emerge in the history of rape. The first is that it is a crime which has always been largely denied. The denial has taken different forms over time, and has changed according to the status of the woman (and that of her attacker). It has varied according to the prevailing perceptions of women and of their role in society. But whatever the time and place, the majority of women never saw their attackers punished. The second theme is the punishment of the victims of rape. For many women, rape was catastrophic not only as a violent assault, but also because of its effect on their reputations and subsequent lives. Illegitimate pregnancies resulted in unemployment, poverty and disease. Worse still, many women were subject to legal condemnation and punishment for the 'crime' of being raped.

DENIALS

RAPE AS A CRIME AGAINST MEN

For much of history rape has been defined as a crime not against the woman attacked, but against the man to whom she belonged (father, guardian, present or future husband). This was the premise in ancient Roman and Jewish law, and persisted in theory in Britain until at least the tenth century (and in practice for a long time thereafter).

Ancient Roman law was unconcerned whether the abductor of an unmarried woman was acting with the consent of his 'victim'. *Raptum* was concerned solely with the abduction of women; it was punishable by death. The seduction of single women, respectable widows and nuns was punished by confiscation of goods or corporal punishment. The seduction of married women was punishable by death. The harsh penalty for *raptum* was directed at the interference with *fathers'* rights, rather than with those of their daughters. Sex (whether consensual or forced) was not a necessary ingredient of the offence. The same offence of *raptum* covered the violent taking of both women and property, and attracted the same penalty whatever the stolen item.

In ancient Jewish laws, the evil at which the offence was directed was that of making impure (and therefore unmarriageable) what was otherwise clean. The penalties for seducing women were, as a result, much the same as those for rape and, like rape, depended upon the marital status of the woman concerned. The seducer, as well as the rapist, of an unattached virgin was punished by marriage to her – he was bound to be responsible for the upkeep of that which he had wrongfully taken. The seducer, as well as the rapist, of an attached woman was punished by death.

The only difference between rape and seduction lay in the woman's punishment. The raped woman was, in theory, free of blame. But the woman who allowed herself to be seduced was punished with death. And whether a woman was taken to have been raped or seduced depended solely upon whether the rape took place inside or outside the city – if the former, a finding of rape could not be made.[1] The woman's offence was committed either at the time of the seduction or when she was found not to be a virgin on her wedding night. Hence a previously single woman would find herself locked into a lifelong marriage with her rapist; and the woman who tried to escape such a fate, by remaining silent about rape, risked execution if she later married and her husband discovered that she was not a virgin.

This perception of rape as a crime against women's keepers shaped English law until the ninth century. The earliest English written law is found in the 'dooms' (statutes) of Æthelberht, King of Kent in the seventh century. The dooms state that a man who 'lies with' a woman who belongs to another man must pay compensation. It seems that the crime was committed whether the woman was a willing participant in sex or not. The compensation depended upon the status of the woman and that of the man to whom she belonged: 'a maiden belonging to the king' attracted 50 shillings in compensation, a 'commoner's serving maid' 12 shillings.[2] If permission had been sought and granted in advance from a woman's owner, it seems that no offence would be committed even if she herself did not consent. If, on the other hand, 'a freeborn woman, with long hair, misconduct[ed] herself', she had to pay 30 shillings compensation.

By the ninth century, English law had developed to the extent that 'rape' as we know it (sex without consent) had appeared in the statutes of King Alfred the Great, and compensation became payable to the woman herself, unless she was a slave. The amount of the compensation still varied, the rape of a commoner was cheaper than that of a noblewoman. However, it seems that the evil of rape was still seen as the reduction of the victim's value, rather than as the attack on her sexual autonomy; any fine was reduced by half if the woman raped was not a virgin; and a non-virgin who willingly had sex with one man when she was engaged to another could be fined twice as much as any man who raped her.

As the years passed and the law developed, rape remained a crime against the woman's keepers. In 1285, and again in 1382, legislation declared that a woman's family could prosecute her 'rapist' even if she 'consented afterwards' or 'forgave him' (loosely translated – if she, but not her family, had consented at the time). And while by the sixteenth century rape had become defined as a sexual offence, concerned with consent rather than with carrying – off, a father's forgiveness of his daughter's rapist was accepted as a bar to prosecution in England until 1774.[3]

RAPE WITHIN MARRIAGE

It was also a legal impossibility for men to rape their wives. So, for example, when Isabella Butler (an heiress) was abducted, forcibly married and raped by William Pull in 1436, she was unable to prosecute her husband until a special Act of Parliament declared that the marriage had been void from the start. It was in the aftermath of this case that Parliament made the abduction of heiresses a crime which, until the eighteenth century, was punished by death. The crime applied only to heiresses, and applied regardless of whether they had chosen to decamp with a lover or been forcibly carried off.

Husbands, however, remained immune from prosecution for rape (in England and Wales) until 1991. Ownership of property includes the right to use it, to abuse it and to destroy it. Since wives were their husbands' property, no wrong was committed when they were physically and sexually abused by their husbands. The murder of women at the hands of their husbands did become recognized as a crime, but until the nineteenth century husbands were free to inflict any injury short of death upon them.

After this time the right of husbands to beat and imprison their wives was curtailed but nowhere was husbands' right to rape their wives restricted. And this right carried with it the right to use such force as was necessary to accomplish the act. By the seventeenth century the right to rape had begun to be defended on grounds other than the husband's ownership of his wife's body. So, for example, Sir Matthew Hale declared in 1678 that 'The husband cannot be guilty of a rape committed by himself upon his lawful wife, for by their mutual matrimonial consent and contract the wife has given up herself in this kind unto her husband, which she cannot retract.[4]

In 1868, John Stuart Mill protested at the freedom of men to rape their wives. For, as he pointed out, even a slave had '(in Christian countries) an admitted right, and is considered under a moral obligation, to refuse to her master the last familiarity. Not so the wife.'[5] (The sentiments were noble, but in fact Mill's perception of the position of slaves was inaccurate. Just as husbands' ownership of their wives gave them the legal right to unhindered sexual access to them, so, in the United States, the owners of slaves remained free to rape them for as long as slavery persisted.) Most ears remained deaf to Mill's protestations, as well as those of many nineteenth-century British and American feminists. In 1924, a man who sued for annulment of his marriage on the grounds of his wife's 'frigidity' (he had never been able to consummate the marriage) was chided by Lord Dunedin for having failed to exhibit 'sufficient virility' by using some 'gentle violence' to achieve consummation by force.[6] The same approach had been taken by the American courts four years before – a man who abstained from intercourse on the grounds that it was painful to his wife was castigated. 'If ... he had the physical power, and refrained from sexual intercourse ... purely out of sympathy for her feelings, he deserves to be doubted for not having asserted his rights.[7]

Commentators in the 1950s poured scorn on the suggestion that wife-rape should be recognized as an offence: 'If a wife is adamant in her refusal, the husband must choose between letting his wife's will prevail, thus wrecking the marriage, and acting without her consent. It would be intolerable', they continued, 'if he were to be conditioned in his course of action by the threat of criminal proceedings.[8] The understanding, on the part of these commentators, was that the decision to rape was a decision to save a marriage. Marriage, in their eyes, could be destroyed by a wife's unwillingness to have sex but not, it seems, by a husband's forcing sex upon her. As late as 1977 English law took the view that 'the wife's consent to sexual intercourse ... [is] implicit in the act of marriage'.[9] While that consent could be revoked by divorce, the bare fact that the husband or wife had left the marriage and even begun proceedings for divorce did not affect it. When the House of Lords, in 1991, convicted a man of the rape of his wife, it did so by overriding the will of Parliament which had been expressed in 1976 and reiterated on several occasions since.

NARROWING THE DEFINITION OF RAPE

Early English law governing unmarried women, and Roman law governing unattached women, denied rape as we know it by defining the offence so widely as to overlook the distinction between free and forced sex (defining free sex as rape). Jewish law denied rape by defining the offence according to where it happened (defining forced sex inside cities as 'non-rape'). And narrow definitions of rape persisted well beyond ancient Jewish times. While ninth-century English law at least accepted the possibility that a non-virgin could be 'thrown down' (although it punished the attack less seriously than one on a virgin), later English law began, at least in practice, to demand virginity as an ingredient of rape. This narrowing of rape's definition coincided with the development of harsh penalties for rape and other criminal offences – the fines of earlier years gave way to execution and mutilation. In the case of rape, the chosen forms of mutilation included castration and blinding. Just as a man who raped a virgin deprived her of her 'member' (hymen), so too would he be deprived of his by castration. Equally, since virgin-rape was caused by the inability to control lust generated by the girl's appearance, blinding would prevent any repeat of the crime. It seems, however, that the man whose eyes led him to rape a woman who was already 'member'-less was undeserving of any punishment. In one case, decided in 1244, a judge rejected a widow's allegation of rape 'because a woman can only [complain] concerning the rape of her virginity'.[10] Not only was rape confined to assaults upon virgins, but it was for centuries assumed that forced sex could not result in pregnancy. In order to qualify as a rape victim, therefore, a woman had to be a virgin who did not conceive as a result of the attack. Ironically, 'rape' required, at times, not only penetration of the vagina by the penis but also actual ejaculation inside the woman's body. The demand for ejaculation by the rapist appears to have come about during the eighteenth century, though by the beginning of the nineteenth century it had been cast into doubt and was soon thereafter abandoned.[11]

By 1275 legislation was passed which stipulated that a woman could be raped regardless of whether she was a virgin or not. At the same time, however, punishment for rape was limited to two years' imprisonment (the penalty for theft was death). And until 1678 'concubinage' operated as a defence to rape; this meant that a man escaped liability for rape if he persuaded a jury that he had slept with the woman, consensually, before.

Developing English law imposed a multitude of procedural requirements with which rape complainants had to comply. The first of these was the 'hue and cry' – the woman who was raped had to go at once to the nearest settlement 'and there show to trustworthy men the injury done to her, and any effusion of blood there may be and any tearing of the clothes'. (Needless to say, these requirements did not apply to other offences.) Once the woman had raised the 'hue and cry', she then had to bring her complaint to *three* criminal courts; if she failed to appear at any one of these courts (the process might take as long as seven years) her complaint was judged false, and the rapist was a free man. In order to succeed she had to repeat, word for word, the precise formula required for a complaint of rape. If she left out any part of it her complaint failed and her attacker was freed. The formula became increasingly complicated with the passing of the years so that, by the thirteenth century, a woman's failure to specify the particular door through which she claimed her attacker had entered her home was sufficient to lead to his acquittal.[12]

By the eighteenth century, virginity or 'good character' on the part of the victim had ceased to be demanded as an ingredient of the rape. The law was still schizophrenic, however, as Blackstone illustrated: 'If the witness be of good fame; if she [quickly reported] the offence, and made great search for the offender; if the party accused fled for it,' her complaint might be true. 'But, on the other hand, if she be of evil fame, and stands unsupported by others, if she concealed the injury for any considerable time after she had the opportunity to complain; if the place, where the fact was alleged to be committed, was where it was possible that she might have been heard and she makes no outcry; there and the like circumstances carry a strong ... presumption that her testimony is false or feigned'.[13] The technical definition of rape had altered but, it seems, the type of rape which might actually lead to a conviction had not. The procedural requirements, the restrictions (first legal, then practical) on the kinds of women who could complain of rape, and the need for ejaculation without resulting pregnancy meant that most rapes were not rapes in the eyes of the English law.

Until 1845 a conviction for rape also required proof that the intercourse had been accomplished by force. Women who wished to complain about rape had to make sure that they received sufficient injuries to qualify. (While this requirement is no longer part of the written law, in practice it still exists, as women who do not receive substantial injury have little chance of securing convictions.) Proof of violence was not required in cases of assault, where lack of resistance could be explained by factors such as the status of the attacker and the youth of the victim.[14] In rape cases, by contrast, actual violence had to be proved over and above that inherent in forced sex itself.

Rape came to be taken more seriously in nineteenth century Britain, but did so in the context of the sexual straitjacketing of Victorian women. Because women were supposed to safeguard their virtue, 'seduction' was expected to include a degree of force. In consequence, women had to fight tooth and nail if they were to be seen as not having consented to sex. In nineteenth-century Wales, many rape complaints were thrown out on the basis that the victim had not resisted sufficiently: 'The popular male presumption, which women had to overcome, was that somehow the latter had encouraged their attackers ... Judges were always looking for signs of "enticement", "prevarication" and "ulterior motive" in rape cases,' even in girls as young as 11.[15]

Medical opinion at the time was that normal healthy women couldn't be forced into sex. As late as 1889 Dr Tait (an influential British doctor) wrote: 'I am perfectly satisfied that no man can effect a felonious purpose on a woman in possession of her senses without her consent'.[16] The very fact that penetration took place (i.e., the very thing that made the assault into 'rape'), was itself seen as proof of eventual consent. So, for example, one court declared in 1860 that the complainant's 'bruises and her protestations merely signified her initial resistance, but *the fact that the assault was consummated* meant that, in the end, [she] consented'.[17]

In the United States, Black women's legal protection from rape was removed entirely in the nineteenth century, when southern

THE CASE FOR TAKING THE DATE OUT OF RAPE

states began to insert the word 'White' before the word 'woman' in the laws on rape. Typical of the time was the decision in State v Charles – the case was dismissed because the charge didn't specify that the victim was White.[18] And in George (a slave) v State (1859), the defendant had his conviction (for raping a Black child less than 10 years old) quashed. According to Mississippi law, slaves had no rights except those specifically granted to them by legislation. Since no statute made the rape of a Black woman criminal, George had committed no offence.[19] But if a slave or a freed Black man raped a White woman, it was a very different story – the death penalty was introduced for such crimes by the southern states during the expansion of slavery. Virginia went so far as to impose the death penalty for the *attempted* rape of a White woman by a Black man in 1823. And discrimination persists – between 1930 and 1977, 89 per cent of men who were executed for rape in the US were Black.[20]

SILENCING WOMEN

The third form of denial which has persisted over time consists of the silencing of women who have been raped. In part, of course, the narrowing of the definition of rape achieves this effect. But women are also silenced when their experiences fall within the legal definitions of rape, but where the penalties for complaining are high.

Perhaps the most obvious penalty for women who complain is the embarrassment, humiliation and shame which many experience. Many women do not report rape because they fear the reaction of their families, lovers, husbands and friends; they also often feel unable to cope with what they perceive as the likely response of the police, particularly where their experience of rape does not match the 'ideal rape'. And there is the fear of the prurient interest of the tabloid press.[21]

But if the stakes in Britain are high today, they used to be a great deal higher. In the past, the identification of a woman with a complaint of rape would devastate her marriage prospects. As a result, many women remained silent. Reluctance to prosecute rape persisted well beyond the Middle Ages, and when cases did get to trial, women were put through the most outrageous humiliations in open court. Until legislation passed in 1828 did away with the need for ejaculation, women were forced to recount their assaults in even more explicit detail than is the case today. Their testimonies were published by the courts and bought for titillation – and all this at a time when the very fact of illicit sex, whether willing or forced, was ruinous for women. Women shamed themselves simply by the complaining about rape. In the nineteenth century, in particular, 'A rape victim's honour, no matter how she struggled, was thought to be irrevocably tarnished according to bourgeois values ... husbands ... sometimes ... viewed rape as a justification for separating from their wives'.[22] This did not prevent the courts from declaring, during this period, that: 'no self-respecting woman, after [being raped] ... can refrain from proclaiming the same to some friend'; and that 'outraged virtue will proclaim her wrong'.[23]

PUNISHING RAPISTS – OR NOT

Yet another form of denial of rape is found in the contrast between the penalties set down by the various laws covering rape and those actually experienced by the small proportion of rapists convicted of their crimes. Seventy-seven per cent of rapists who were convicted between 1066 and 1208 were punished only by being fined; this during a period when most criminal offences were punished by mutilation or death.[24] The official penalty for rape at the time was at least castration, or occasionally execution. Most cases, however, were settled by the marriage of victim and attacker or by a payment of cash or land. No records of individual cases exist before the 1190s. But as soon as records do become available, the gulf between theory and practice becomes apparent. Of all reported rape prosecutions between

1194 and 1216, not a single defendant was punished for the alleged attack.[25] Throughout the whole of the thirteenth century, in fact, only one case has ever been found in which a sentence of mutilation appears actually to have been imposed. Even this is disputed.[26] And although a mandatory death penalty for rape existed between 1285 and 1321, not a single case can be found in which a man was actually executed. Those men who were found guilty were able to buy pardons or, failing this, were generally subject only to imprisonment, minor fines or marriage to their victims. Still, women continued to be imprisoned for technical irregularities in their complaints.

Not only were punishments relatively light, but many more men were acquitted than convicted. It seems that the very availability of harsh physical penalties for rape made juries eager to seize on the most spurious reasons to acquit. It was also common for men to be convicted of lesser offences than those with which they were charged. Rape, even in theory, attracted severe penalties only if classified as a felony (serious crime). Juries could decide to acquit of felony on the basis of any imperfection in procedure but, nevertheless, to convict of a trespass if they believed the woman's claim. Trespasses were punishable only by a fine.

This practice of convicting rapists of trespass rather than felony should have died out in 1285, when new legislation required that all rapes be defined as felonies. It is likely that one motive behind the legislation was greed on the part of the state. While fines imposed for felonies were paid to the state, those imposed for trespasses were paid to the victim. But, far from increasing the conviction and punishment rates for men accused of rape, it seems that juries used any excuse to avoid subjecting men even to the possibility of serious punishment. It was after this time that failure to specify such details as the door through which an attacker was alleged to have entered began to be sufficient to acquit the man and lead to the woman's conviction for 'false complaint'.[27] At least, in such cases, the king got his pound of flesh.

What was true of medieval England was also true of Italy in the late-fourteenth and early-fifteenth centuries. Again, despite the availability of death and mutilation as punishments for rape, the penalties actually experienced by convicted rapists were mild. Except where men were found guilty of raping the very young or very elderly, or where rape crossed the social boundaries of Renaissance society, little concern was displayed. Men were typically allowed to choose between a few months' imprisonment, a fine or, if she was unwed, marriage to their victim. But if a man raped his social superior, or was convicted of sodomy (whether consensual or forced), a very much sterner attitude was taken.[28]

As time passed, it does seem that the severity of punishment for rape increased. Between the sixteenth and nineteenth centuries, men in England were executed for rape. In Middlesex and London, for example, 55 per cent of men convicted of rape were executed between 1576 and 1804. It is not until one looks at the total numbers concerned that the impression of severity falls away. In these densely-populated areas, over the space of 230 years, 19 men were executed for rape. In comparison, in the space of just 22 years (1749–1771) in the same two counties 584 people were executed for offences against property.[29] Those men who were hanged for rape tended to be those who had typically been caught with their pants down, in circumstances where there could be no doubt about their victims' lack of consent. Also, they tended to be men who were themselves despised – soldiers, hangmen, those who had killed or horribly injured as well as raped.[30] The severity of their punishments was utterly out of character with the norm.

PUNISHING WOMEN

I have concentrated in this chapter on the ways in which the crime of rape has been denied; my final point concerns the overt punishment of women who were raped, either by the law or, more generally, by society. In the first century AD it was common practice throughout Europe for 'adulteresses' to be drowned in mire. Rape victims were similarly treated, and the practice continued in England until the sixth or early-seventh century.[31] But while the practice of killing rape victims died out, the practice of punishing them did not. As late as the nineteenth century, complainants who could not provide a surety (a sum of money, similar to bail, then required from both accused and accuser) were imprisoned in order to ensure that they appeared at the trial. In one case in 1800, a 14-year-old girl spent a month in solitary confinement on bread and water (her father could not afford the surety) while the lawyer accused of raping her walked free on bail. Women whose rapes were interrupted could be charged with indecent exposure, and those whose attackers were acquitted were frequently charged with perjury.[32]

If a woman did brave making a complaint and then, for whatever reason, failed to get her attacker convicted, she was automatically guilty of 'false appeal' and was subject to imprisonment and a fine. One study of cases tried across England between 1208 and 1321 shows that 49 per cent of women were imprisoned as a result of their allegations. Only 15 per cent of the accused men were punished for rape itself.[33]

Women who complied with the rules by reporting rape at once were imprisoned for false allegation if they became pregnant – because it was assumed that rape couldn't cause pregnancy – and women who waited to see if they were pregnant before reporting rape were imprisoned for failure to follow the proper procedures. In addition, those women who decided (or whose fathers decided) to make the most of the mess by marrying their rapists could find themselves penalized by a fine if the marriage took place after the rape had been reported.

Concentrating primarily upon the later years, perhaps the most significant danger for women who were raped was that of pregnancy. It has already been noted, above, that rapes were not considered capable of resulting in pregnancy. As a result, the pregnant woman was invariably a 'fallen woman', rather than the victim of an offence. In the eighteenth century half of all women in London who were aged between 16 and 25 were in domestic service.[34] Servants were dependent upon their employers not only for wages, but also for their homes. And it was not unusual for the master of the household (or for one or more of his sons), to take his pick of the more attractive household servants.

Such behaviour was not viewed as rape at the time – any maid who complained of it would be viewed as a strumpet whose motive was gain. But a pregnant maid was a fallen woman who would be thrown out of employment and home. In the event that any genuine fondness for her was felt by her 'seducer', she might find herself looked after, at least for a time. More commonly, she would find herself on the street. If she survived the pregnancy long enough to give birth to a live baby, the law held her financially responsible for its upkeep. Technically the responsibility was shared between her and the father but, given the impossibility of proving paternity, the responsibility was hers alone (and in 1834 the law changed to reflect reality – a new Poor Law relieved men from any responsibility for the upkeep of their illegitimate offspring).

If the mother was fortunate enough to find another job, the child would be taken into care and she would be charged for its upkeep. If she was unable to pay, the child became the responsibility of the parish in which she lived and the mother was incarcerated in the workhouse. If the woman concealed her pregnancy and the child was born dead or (as was not uncommon at the time) succumbed to some childhood illness, she was presumed to have killed it and, between 1624 and 1803, would have been executed.

Women who were raped by their masters, then, took full responsibility for the offence. There was little chance of prosecution, and the burden of resulting pregnancies fell to them alone. Financial responsibility for the child was linked with such social condemnation for the 'sin' as to make it impossible for most to earn a living other than as prostitutes. This, together with execution on suspicion of infanticide or for offences connected with prostitution, was woman's punishment.

Women who were physically overpowered without a struggle, or who were paralysed with fear by their attackers, did not qualify as victims of rape. Perhaps the crowning irony in this brief history of rape is that those who did struggle could find themselves punished for assault. One such woman was Mary Weimar, who was imprisoned in London in 1825. Mary had been attacked by a man and had fought him off in 'a spirit of resistance to his unmanly attacks'.[35] This was precisely the behaviour expected of women who were threatened with rape. The trouble was, it seems, that Mary's attacker, rather than Mary herself, ended up with serious injuries. Mary was found guilty of assault, and imprisoned for three months despite having already spent time in prison while awaiting trial. Her attacker was not punished at all.

PART 2

The Case

3

The Birth of Date Rape

DATE RAPE ARRIVES IN BRITAIN

It was the trial of Austen Donnellan in 1993 which brought 'date rape' onto Britain's front pages. Donnellan was accused of rape by a friend with whom he had sex after a party. She was very drunk at the time. She said that she woke up to find him having sex with her; he claimed she was a willing partner. Donnellan was acquitted after the woman accepted in court that she couldn't remember what had happened, so that Donnellan's account of events 'might have happened'.[1]

Donnellan's lawyer called the trial 'the uniquest criminal case ever'. The press reeled with amazement that a woman who got into bed with a man could later bring a rape charge against him. Editorials pondered the (apparently fine) line between rape and bad manners, and men complained that rape accusations had become an occupational hazard for the sexually active.

When Donnellan was acquitted, the popular press clamoured for changes to the law. As it stood, Donnellan's accuser could remain anonymous while *his* name was published far and wide. The *Daily Mail* called for the woman to be named. Tory MP Geoffrey Dickens demanded that rape complainants be identified 'where the courts rejected their stories',[2] and over two thousand *Sun* readers rang the newspaper to agree. Sir Nicholas Fairbairn called for all rape complainants to be named because, he claimed, most complaints of rape are false.[3] In the end, the Government decided to leave the law as it was. But the public was left in little doubt that the anonymity which currently cloaks alleged rape victims amounts to an undeserved privilege for hordes of scheming and unscrupulous liars.

In fact, rape complainants were granted anonymity (in 1976) because so *few* of them came forward to report (rape is still the most under-reported serious crime). The fact that a man is acquitted of rape does *not* mean that his accuser was lying. In the *Donnellan* case, for example, the woman couldn't remember what had happened. She might have been asleep, or simply too drunk to remember. But either way, the jury *had* to acquit, because if she couldn't remember, there was nothing to base a guilty verdict on. The case was probably too weak ever to come to court. But then, it wasn't the woman who had wanted it to – Donnellan himself had in order to clear his name.

Whatever the niceties of this, the press went wild because the woman who had accused Donnellan of rape was not a stranger who claimed to have been jumped on in the street. Not only was she a friend who had kissed him on several occasions (including, in public, on the night of the alleged rape), but she had also gone home and got into bed with him. This, at last, was a home-grown date rape – a subject which had obsessed the United States since the trials of William Kennedy Smith and Mike Tyson in 1991 and 1992. And this version of 'date rape' was even better than the American variety – it involved two people who were actually in bed together!

Hardly had the Donnellan case cleared the headlines than Angus Diggle was tried for attempting to rape a fellow solicitor after a ball. Diggle was convicted. In yet another case, Matthew Kydd, like Austen Donnellan, was acquitted of raping a fellow student. His acquittal seemed inevitable once the jury were told that she was known at college as 'slut of the year'. And, as the first anniversary of the date rape hysteria passed, David Warren and Ben Emerson (both students) were acquitted of raping the women who had taken them to bed. A judge dismissed the Warren case himself. Despite the fact that the woman said no, her 'no' had not, according to the judge, been sufficiently 'emphatic', and she had not resisted physically.[4] The judge who presided over a jury's acquittal of Ben Emerson heartily congratulated them on their verdict, despite the fact that Emerson had admitted to the police that the woman (who had invited him home for a massage) hadn't consented to penetrative sex.[5]

Every date rape acquittal now results in complaints that such cases ever get to court, and in demands that the men's identities are kept secret. When David Warren was acquitted, the *Daily Telegraph* reported accusations that the Crown Prosecution Service was 'too ready to bring rape cases to court with a level of evidence that would dissuade them from proceeding with any other kind of offence'. One lawyer was quoted as saying that she believed the CPS felt pressurized 'by women's groups and by media publicity to go ahead with prosecutions based on the evidence of one woman against one man'.[6] This was, she obviously thought, a very bad thing.

How else one wonders, can rapists *ever* be convicted? It is possible to prove that a man had sex with a woman (he will leave traces of sperm, skin and/or pubic hair that can be matched by means of DNA testing). But you can't prove non-consent by *physical* evidence. And so the only rape cases that wouldn't depend on 'her word against his' are those that took place in public. Such cases, it hardly needs to be said, are unusual. Naturally, however, mere details such as this did not prevent the same uproar from following the acquittals of policeman Michael Seear in February 1995, and of actor Craig Charles the following month.

Press indignation at the 'outrage' perpetrated on these men extends even to convicted offenders. Solicitor Angus Diggle was found guilty of the attempted rape of a woman he had taken to a ball. They had not been sexually involved, but had had to share a bed at a friend's flat after the ball. She undressed and got into bed. Diggle took off his clothes and tried to have sex with her. Afterwards he demanded of the police: 'I have spent £200 on her. Why can't I do what I did to her?' An appeal judge later remarked that Diggle had shown no remorse for the episode: 'He regards himself as the victim'.[7] Geoffrey Wheatcroft agreed with Diggle: he, together with Mike Tyson in the US, 'might be called victims of society ... Nowadays, when a lovely woman stoops to folly she calls it rape.'[8]

Minette Marrin went further. When Diggle was released from jail in September 1994, Marrin proclaimed him worthy of 'the heartfelt sympathy of anybody with any sense'. Diggle, she raged, was 'subjected to a most disgraceful injustice ... unjustly convicted ... The whole date-rape nonsense, of which this is the worst example in this country, was the direct result of political correctness.'[9]

So just what is this 'date-rape nonsense'? The only thing that distinguishes date rape from any other rape is the context in which it takes place. In England and Wales rape is sex that takes place without the consent of the woman, when the man knows that she is not or may not be consenting. A woman who says no to sex indicates that she does not consent to it.

In all the British cases mentioned so far, the women claimed that the defendants had behaved in ways that fitted the legal definition of rape (or attempted rape). What made the allegations special, what made them into allegations of date rape, was simply that the men and women involved had been in each others' company willingly, in social contexts, in situations with at least the potential for sexual contact. In most of the cases, the man and woman were sharing a bed (or about to) when the alleged assault happened, and there had been some consensual sexual contact before the disputed incident.

It is not surprising that few such cases reach the courts. If a woman gets into bed with a man, or even if she just allows herself to be alone with him, any forced sex that takes place will be very difficult for her to prove. No one will have seen what happened, and probably no one will have heard. And if one or both of them has taken off any clothes before the assault, he can penetrate her very quickly indeed – she can be caught off guard, without any struggle, and with no resulting physical evidence of bruising and so on. If this happens it is unlikely that she will shout 'rape' and start to scream – typically, shock and embarrassment act as an effective gag. Even when rape occurs in much less intimate circumstances, it will usually be very difficult to prove. If a woman invites a man in for a drink after a date, or agrees to his request for coffee after he walks her home from a party, there may be no one nearby to hear her cry out if he pounces. But more than any of this, his claim that she consented to sex is very much more plausible than if he was a stranger who had jumped her in the street.

Small wonder, then, that there have been few date rape convictions. Yet the issue has spawned several television programmes, a great number of column inches, and the revision of many university disciplinary procedures after Donnellan's college attempted (unsuccessfully) to handle the rape allegation itself.

In 1990 Oxford University's Students Union published the report of an investigation into sexual harassment. The investigators, it seems, got more than they bargained for when they found that sexual harassment in the university included incidents of rape. The difficulties faced by the women concerned were indicated by the wry remark of one of the survey's authors: 'Most dons would only believe a rape had happened here if it was in broad daylight in the front quad with the whole Senior Common Room as witnesses.'[10]

At about the same time came Kate Painter's nationwide survey of married women. She found that one in seven had been raped by their husbands,[11] a figure which reflected almost exactly the findings of Diane Russell's 1978 survey in California.[12] The *Guardian* pointed out that, if the British results were extrapolated across the country, almost one and a half million women had been raped by their husbands or ex-husbands. Rape in marriage was not yet a crime.[13]

In March and August 1991 *Cosmopolitan* magazine carried a number of articles on date rape. Between March and June of that year over 300 women wrote to the magazine saying they had been raped by men they knew. Shortly afterwards, the results of the Cambridge University Students Union survey showed that one in nine student women had been raped, and that 1 in 5 had experienced attempted rape. The attackers were usually men they knew.

EXPLAINING THE RISE IN DATE RAPE

The term 'date rape' was coined in the United States to bring home to women that forced sex was rape even if it took place in the context of a 'date'. Inasmuch as it performed this function it was a useful term. But the danger in it was that sceptics would seize on the 'date' in 'date rape' to suggest that what women experienced as forced intercourse in this context was not what the law should recognize as rape. This is, in fact, what has happened. The message almost unanimously trumpeted by the press is that date rape is not about forced sexual intercourse. It is about something else – sex secured by emotional pressure, drunken flings, morning-after regrets – which whingeing women want to define as rape. Criticism focuses on the apparent explosion in the frequency with which such rape is alleged. There was a time when rapes that were complained of usually involved strangers. Now the rapes about which women speak frequently involve dates, friends, lovers and husbands. So, the commentators reason, either the incidence of rape has increased to an utterly unbelievable extent, or women are calling rape what they used to call a drunken fling or bad sex. The general conclusion of the press is that the definition of rape has expanded beyond all reason as a result of loony feminist action about date rape.

Let's look at what really happened. In January 1971, the New York Radical Feminists held a 'Rape Speak-out', at which women talked about their experiences of rape. A conference on rape followed in April. '*The central revelation*,' according to the organizers, 'was that the violent rapist and the boyfriend/husband are one. The friend and lover commits rape every bit as much as the "fiend" prowling the street.'[14] The discoveries that women were, by and large, raped by men they knew, and that rape was much more common than people had previously supposed, directly challenged the popular stereotype of rape. Until then, people's understanding of the crime was shaped only by the offences that were reported; these almost invariably involved strangers who attacked women either on the street or after having broken into their homes, and who left their victims seriously injured. The courts were reluctant to convict rapists who did not fit within this category. The police, in turn, were slow to prosecute them and, very often, refused even to record alleged rapes as crimes. The message then trickled back to women who, when attacked by men they knew, often did not even define forced sex as rape.

The discovery of non-stranger rape carried its own momentum. The more studies that were carried out the more aware women became of sexual violence; the more aware women became, the more they were prepared to share their stories and to campaign for improvement; the more women campaigned, the more interest there was in gathering statistics about the incidence of rape; the more studies were carried out, the more apparent it became that rape was very common and was, on the whole, committed by men known to their victims. The University of Michigan, for example, established a Rape Crisis Centre in 1986. In 1985 there had been three reported rapes. In 1989 over 100 rapes were reported in the university. Students in a number of other institutions took direct action by scrawling 'rape lists' on bathroom walls. The universities instituted complaint and hearing procedures as a result.

So, there is a certain truth in the claim that the apparent increase in the incidence of rape is explained (at least in part) by a redefinition of the offence. But it is vital to understand the nature of that redefinition. Far from rape being expanded to cover every episode of drunken sex, every unsatisfactory one-night stand, the understanding of rape has been extended beyond the atypical 'ideal' rape, to include all cases where men force sex upon women who, to their knowledge, are not consenting. This extension, then, goes no further than the current legal definition of rape in the United Kingdom.

RAPE AND THE LAW

The transition from theory to action, from the collection of 'forced sex' statistics to the prosecution of individuals, marked another stage in rape's apparent increase. As women became more aware of the problem of non-stranger rape, the pressure grew for these attacks to result in prosecution and conviction. There were a number of legal hurdles to overcome. In Britain the major problem lay not in the definition of rape, but in police practice. Non-stranger rape was not treated seriously. In the United States the definitions of rape adopted by many states did create problems for women; certain legal rules and practices meant that women who were raped by men they knew had little, if any, chance of seeing their attackers convicted. The three most obvious examples of this were the fact that it was not possible to define wife-rape as a crime; the requirement for resistance on the part of the victim; and the requirement of corroboration (that is, independent evidence, such as a witness).15 In the 1970s it was possible for one commentator to define rape as 'unlawful sexual intercourse between a male and a female, not the wife of the perpetrator, under circumstances that render the female legally incapable of consenting to the act; or where the female's resistance to the act is overcome by force or violence, or threats of bodily harm.16 By 1990, as a result of feminist pressure, all but six US states had made wife-rape criminal, although only a third did so entirely without exception.17 The rest either had a special category of 'marital sexual assault', or required either that the couple had begun divorce proceedings, legally separated or stopped living together.

Wife rape may not appear directly relevant to date rape. But as long as any man is immune from rape charges because of his relationship with his victim, all rapists are judged in part on the basis of their previous relationships with their victims. If we judge husbands to be entirely free from legal blame, we reduce the guilt attributed to ex-husbands, lovers, boyfriends, friends and acquaintances, and we do so because of their relationships with the women they rape. The removal of husbands' immunity from rape charges led to an increase in the number of reported and prosecuted rapes.

Wherever the resistance requirement formed part of the law, it applied in theory to all charges of rape. In practice, however, the courts required very different levels of resistance depending on the relationship between the victim and the attacker, and upon the colours of their skin.18 If the court regarded the man as an obviously unsuitable sexual partner for the women (whether because of his race, social class or the circumstances in which the attack took place), little resistance would be demanded from her. But if he was regarded as someone to whom she might consent the courts demanded superhuman efforts of resistance from the woman before any conviction was possible. Gradually, resistance requirements were made less stringent. 'Utmost resistance' was replaced by 'reasonable resistance' in some states, and the focus moved to the defendants' use or threat of force. Convictions became more possible and women became more prepared to come forward. While actual convictions in such cases remain a rarity, women do sometimes make reports to the police and, occasionally, get as far as the criminal courts. This, coupled with the obsessive media focus on all things 'sexual' has the effect that these cases appear to be on the increase.

The third significant legal change that contributed to the apparent rise in date rape was the gradual dismantling of the *corroboration* requirement in the rape laws of many US states. Until relatively recently, women could not get convictions in rape cases unless there was independent evidence, over and above their word, of all the essential ingredients of rape. In theory, women had to provide additional independent evidence not only of the identity of their alleged attacker and the fact of sexual intercourse, but also of their non-consent and/or the use of force.

Women who were raped by men they knew found it extraordinarily hard to comply with the corroboration requirements. Since such rapes typically take place indoors and away from potential witnesses, it will generally be impossible to provide evidence of non-consent and/or force and/or resistance unless physical injury occurs. Even if there were marks of physical force, they might be consistent with consensual, rough-and-tumble sex. The corroboration rule, like the resistance requirement, applied in theory to all rape cases. Like the resistance requirement, its impact was felt much more in cases involving potentially 'suitable' male sexual partners.

The abolition of the absolute requirement for corroboration in many US states meant that rapes which could not previously have been prosecuted could now be brought to court. As with the change to the resistance rule, the abolition of the corroboration requirement did not much increase the chances of conviction. Jurors remain extremely unlikely to believe a woman who states that she was raped in circumstances in which, or by someone with whom, she might 'suitably' have engaged in consensual sex. Nevertheless, where this remains a matter for the jury rather than a rule of law, the chances of getting a complaint as far as the courtroom are increased, even if the chances of conviction remain negligible. Again, this has the effect that the incidence of rape appears to increase.

To return the focus to Britain; in both the Ben Emerson and Austen Donnellan cases, if the jury had believed the women's stories, they should have convicted the defendants. Both men were accused of having sex with the women *without their consent*, and lack of consent is the central element of rape in English law. Obviously such rapes (had they been committed) would not have been as serious as those perpetrated by men who threaten their victims or who terrorize them into submission. But the fact that an alleged offence does not qualify as the most serious possible example of the relevant crime isn't usually taken to mean that the alleged victim is a scheming harlot, or the alleged offender is the victim of a miscarriage of justice.

Men who find themselves on the receiving end of crime are likely to have been victimized in public. They will have been set upon on the way home from the pub or robbed in the street, for example. The public nature of these crimes makes it likely that they will come to the attention of the police and, if the offender can be traced, of the courts.

Women's victimization, by contrast, generally takes place in private. Our attackers are usually the men we know. Half of all women who are murdered die at the hands of their husbands – many more are beaten and raped. This violence is hidden still, and its absence from the legal sphere has shaped the way in which we think about crime. The demands from women that these private crimes be recognized have the potential to subvert our whole understanding of 'crime', and also to threaten relationships between the sexes. It is this which provokes the cries of denial.

THE BIRTH OF DATE RAPE

The Forms of Denial in the Media

An article in *Playboy* of October 1990 complained that the definition of rape to cover dating situations 'gives women a simple way of thinking about sex that externalizes guilt, remorse or conflict. Bad feelings after sex becomes someone else's fault. A sexual encounter is transformed into a one-way event in which the woman has no stake, no interest and no active role. Assuming the status of victim is in many ways an easy answer – but not one befitting a supposedly liberated woman.'1

Many journalists would not usually wish to identify themselves with *Playboy*'s stance, but in fact the attitude expressed in the piece is a very common one. In *Not Guilty: In Defence of the Modern Man* David Thomas assures his readers that the real meaning of statistics which suggest that between one in three and one in two of US college women will experience rape or some other sexual assault is 'not just that some college girls will be the victims of genuine assaults, but that lots of co-eds will have bad nights and will then wake up the next morning with a sore head, look at the guy lying next to them and think, "Oh, Shit"'. There seems to be little way he suggests, 'in which a boy can avoid being accused of rape.'[2] Thomas insists that women must take responsibility for sex: 'I would not condone any acts of brutality or unreasonable coercion. But women cannot be raunchy sex kittens on the one hand and delicate virgins on the other. If they want to be as free as men, they may have to accept that they will end up being as unprotected.'[3] Thomas puts himself forward as a 'modern man'; but his argument is as old as the hills, and deeply conservative. Women who complain of sexual assault have always been categorized as 'madonna' or 'whore'. At times in the past, only virgins could complain of rape at all. To this day, women's sexual experiences with other men are often used in court to discredit them and to suggest that they consented to sex with their attackers. There is little new, therefore, in Thomas' distinction between 'delicate virgin' and 'raunchy sex kitten'. But he goes further in trying to sell this distinction to the 'sex kittens' as well as to the 'delicate virgins' – his argument is supposed to appeal to feminists as well as to their more conservative sisters. It isn't as if he is denying protection to 'raunchy sex kittens' in order to *punish* them – he's simply pointing out that the notion of such protection is outdated and insulting.

The argument that sexual equality requires that women are denied protection from men is, of course, a nonsense. Women tend to be physically weaker than men, and can generally be overpowered by them. The law cannot actually prevent such assaults but it can, if properly applied, punish the offenders. To remove such laws would leave us *less* equal, *more* vulnerable to assault by men. But it wouldn't change men's lack of vulnerability to assault by women, as this depends not on legal rules but on physiological fact.

If the views of David Thomas appear extreme, however, they are mild in comparison with those of Sir Nicholas Fairbairn (recently deceased Tory MP and, at one time, Scotland's senior lawyer).

THE FORMS OF DENIAL IN THE MEDIA

Throwing caution to the wind in a 1994 debate on rape the MP demanded: 'Are women so feeble that they have to be protected? Not at all, they are the tauntresses.' Claiming that women are not victims, but rather active participants, he goes on: 'She may complain, if you allow her to be the victim – it's an easy part to play ... Every time we say women are in some way feeble and victims ... it is not only an insult to women but also an encouragement to cry rape.'[4]

Sir Nicholas appears to mean one of two things. Either he is stating that sex can't happen unless women want it to, and that to claim otherwise is to treat us as physically 'feeble' and thereby to insult us; or he is claiming that since 'women', as a category, participate willingly in sex (even if only with their husbands), *all* women, simply by virtue of *being* women, are *always* willing to have sex with *any* man. All sex is, therefore, consensual, and *no* woman can *ever* be raped.

It is not difficult to point out how absurd these arguments are. As far as the first is concerned, you only have to consider the likely outcome of a struggle between Miss Black Rhode Island and Mike Tyson. She was, in the words of one commentator, 'an 18-year-old, 108-pound woman in a hotel room with a person who could arguably be considered the best fighter of all time.'[5] Small wonder she was terrified. To accept that she could physically be overpowered by such a man is hardly to insult women (I, for one, am not insulted). As for the second, accepting the actuality of rape can only enfeeble women as a group if rape is defined as sex to which women *consent*. If we were to include as 'rape' sex in which a woman participated willingly but later regretted, this would truly infantilize women, by denying us the responsibility for making up our minds at the time. But if we define rape as sex to which a woman did not consent at the time, we are not treating women as feeble. We are, on the contrary, upholding the right of women to be sexually autonomous.

THE CASE FOR TAKING THE DATE OUT OF RAPE

Sir Nicholas may have held extreme views, but more pernicious is the more 'reasonable' approach adopted by many commentators which accepts that women are sometimes raped, views rape as a 'vicious and unmanly crime', and demands that rapists should be 'dealt with harshly. Prison is one way, castration another.' In tandem with this condemnation, however, is generally an insistence that the term 'rape' should not be used promiscuously. Michael Vermeulen, for example, warned that: 'Crying "rape" when what you should be saying is "what did I do?" is not going to get anyone anywhere. In fact, the loose application of the term by in-your-face feminists not only demeans the suffering of real rape victims, it fosters an attitude of powerlessness among women (and hostility among men) that may be politically correct but is bad for society.'[6]

David Thomas adopts a similar position; he accepts that there is a 'horrifying, but still small, possibility of *random* assault', but goes on to ask: 'Why should college girls need to be protected from their peers?' He suggests that 'the date-rape panic isn't about real incidents of violence; it's about a fear of sex.'[7]

The message from both these men is that 'real violence' involves 'random assault' (remember Little Red Riding Hood). The flip side of this coin is that non-random assault is about sex, not rape. Hence when a woman is forcibly penetrated by her husband, this is a 'domestic dispute'. When a student is pinned down and penetrated by a man to whom she has offered floor-space for the night, this is a 'misunderstanding'. The process of relabelling serves to obscure the fact of forced sex, and the incidents can then be understood as events for which both the men and the women bear responsibility.

Kate Roiphe achieved a certain fame with her book *The Morning After*. In this she too argues that date rape is really sex which is regretted, and that women who complain of it are reneging on their own sexual responsibilities. She cites a number of texts to back up her argument. She quotes Catherine McKinnon: 'Politically, I call it rape whenever a woman has sex with a man and feels violated.' She cites a discussion of 'verbal coercion' so as to suggest that 'verbal coercion' is widely accepted as sufficient to make a man guilty of rape ('verbal coercion' being defined to include 'verbal arguments not including verbal threats of force'). 'If verbal coercion constitutes rape', Roiphe protests, 'then the word rape itself expands to include any kind of sex a woman experiences as negative.'[8] Roiphe gives the impression that men are actually being criminalized simply for making 'women feel violated', for engaging in 'verbal coercion'. The reader is left with a picture of men imprisoned for obtaining sex by means of tactics such as 'I really love you darling'; 'If you loved me you would'; 'If you don't, I'll go and have sex with Jane instead.'

Two separate issues are being deliberately confused here. At one level women are talking about unwanted sex; at another, they are talking about rape. Rape is sex to which women *do not consent*: unwanted sex, by contrast, may be consented to for a variety of reasons. Women may want to please their partners in order to escape criticism, sulks or the poverty which frequently follows divorce; they may decide that they can't be bothered to argue with a man they have taken to their beds with no intention of having penetrative sex; they may feel obliged to have sex in order to prevent their boyfriends or husbands turning to other women for sexual satisfaction; they may want to remain in joyless marriages for the sake of their children.

It is perhaps unfortunate that sex is not always joyful, spontaneous and equally desired by both participants. But it is a fact of life that we decide to do some things that we do not particularly desire to do. If a woman chooses unwanted sex in preference to sulks, abandonment, coldness, criticism or causing hurt or offence to her partner, she consents to that sex. If her partner is aware of that choice he may be accused of insensitivity, selfishness and a lack of regard for her. But he cannot be accused of rape.

On the other side of the coin, however, are the women who 'choose' sex in preference to a beating; the women whose physical struggles are overridden by the men who decide to have sex with them anyway; the women whose verbal 'no's are ignored by men who misread their 'body language'; the women who are frozen into passivity by the fear of injury or death; the women who are penetrated when unconscious. When any of these women complain of rape (and most of them do not) they are not attempting to abdicate their responsibility for sex. Kate Roiphe claims: 'We like to think of men as the aggressors and ourselves as victims because it allows us to surrender responsibility in a time of sexual ambiguity, suspicion and danger.'[9] In fact, women who complain of rape do so *precisely* because the responsibility has been taken away from them.

Of course there are difficult nuances here. In every case where a choice is made between one evil (unwanted sex) and another evil (loss of a boyfriend, poverty, physical injury or even death), it is possible to define the choice of the lesser evil (here, unwanted sex), as consent. Traditionally, women have been praised if they valued their chastity more highly than their lives (the Catholic church, in particular, has made a business out of creating saints of women who were killed in exactly these circumstances). But few would claim that a woman who chooses sex in preference to death could be said to have consented in a way which should prevent that sex from being defined as rape.

Those who claim that date rape isn't rape make much of the fact that many women who reported forced sex with non-strangers in these studies did not (at least initially) define their experiences as 'rape'. Minette Marrin, writing in the *Sunday Telegraph* takes evident relish in this fact. Referring to testimonies in *Cosmopolitan* from numerous women who said that they had not at first recognized their experiences of forced sex as rape, Marrin remarks: 'Call me old-fashioned, but I think that if I were raped, I would probably notice it at the time.'[10] No doubt if Marrin was leapt upon by a stranger she would use the word rape. Many women, however, have trouble in applying the term to forced sex with a friend or lover. Diane Russell's 1970s study of wife rape uncovered 87 women who had been raped by their husbands. Only six of these women answered 'yes' to a direct question relating to rape. But all 87 reported attacks which fitted the legal definition of rape (forced penetrative sex) when they were questioned about sexual *abuse* by their husbands.[11] And David Finkelhor and Kersti Yllo, who conducted a separate survey, found a similar reluctance on the part of women to identify themselves as raped. They suggest two possible reasons for this. In the first place, 'Stranger rape imagery so dominates our understanding of the word "rape" that sexual assaults by intimates often do not fit the picture.' Secondly, 'The word "rape" has powerful connotations, suggesting a grievous violation, moral outrage, crime, punishment, police and so forth. Many women do not want, or are not ready, to attach such connotations to their experience.'[12] Particularly where the relationship continued, the refusal to label an assault as rape can be a temporary form of damage limitation.

The irony in the positions adopted by Roiphe, Marrin, Thomas *et al.* is that it is they *themselves* who expand the term to cover all sex about which women complain. So unwilling are they to recognize that many women are subjected to forced sex by their partners that, they tell us, the statistics *must* refer simply to less-than-marvellous sex. Then, bizarrely, they accuse *feminists* of extending the meaning of rape to cover consented-to sex.

Why do such critics assume that consent has been given in situations where women later allege date rape? Consent is assumed from the circumstances in which such rapes occur. Consent isn't confined to agreement (whether spoken or unspoken) to the particular act of sex. It is a much wider thing than this. It can be found in a woman's previous behaviour, whether with this man or another. It can be found in her talking to, or smiling at, or flirting with or kissing the man who later attacks her. It can even be found in her reputation, or in the relationship of friend, date, colleague or acquaintance. It doesn't matter whether she wanted the *particular* act of sex on that *particular* occasion with that *particular* man – her consent, as it is understood by the critics of date rape, has already been given.

This is of course outrageous. And what is even more outrageous is that the people who espouse this attitude tell women who complain of date rape that *they* are being 'sexually conservative'. There is *nothing* more conservative than the attitude that women consent to sex by smiling, or flirting, or wearing short dresses. This is the attitude that gives men permission to rape, and it is the attitude that lets them get away with it.

Another of the pernicious trivializations of date rape promulgated in the media is the assumption that sex forced on a woman by someone she knows (however slightly) is simply a less serious assault than sex forced on her by a stranger. It seems that the assumption operates both in relation to the woman's reaction, and to the man's degree of blameworthiness. David Thomas, for example, treats his readers to a tragic tale of how an ex-girlfriend made a pass at him and then refused to follow through: 'It took about five years, a fair amount of analysis and more love than I deserved to turn me back into an emotionally functioning human being.' His sense of self-esteem must have been fragile indeed, that mere sexual rejection could so bring him to his knees. Nevertheless, Thomas goes on to advise us that 'Many people, male and female, are devastated by the everyday wounds of love, yet we consider their pain, no matter how deep or long lasting, far less than that of a woman who happens to have had sex on an occasion when she did not wish to have it.'[13]

It is not true that people generally see unwanted sex itself as a worse ill than the pain of rejection. For many people, unwanted sex is an everyday fact of life. But it is true that many would consider it worse to be *raped* than to have our sexual advances turned down. To have the latter happen is to be denied something to which we have no claim in the first place. We can hope and wish that our sexual attractions are mutual, but we are hardly in a position to complain if they are not. To be raped, however, is to be treated as non-human in a very fundamental way. We may not be able to make many positive demands about what happens to us (these demands require resources and cooperation from others). But we can at least expect the power of veto over what goes into our bodies, what becomes part of ourselves.

Rape is no less damaging just because you know your attacker. Instead of categorizing the seriousness of the attack in terms of the relationship between the man and the woman, we should be looking at the fear, the injury, the threat and the resulting harm. In many ways it may be worse to be raped by someone you know. If you are attacked by a stranger while hitchhiking in France, for example, you can refuse to hitchhike in France again. If you are attacked by a stranger on your doorstep you can move house. But if you are attacked by a trusted friend, or an apparently attractive man with whom you have shared a few drinks, how can you make sure it doesn't happen again?

Date rape is further trivialized by the widespread assumption that such rapes do not involve violence. Fairly typical was the response of Ted Brown of the Libertarian Party of Los Angeles County to California's withdrawal of bail from men accused of rape: 'We don't want rapists prowling the street ... [but t]his would affect people who potentially are not violent offenders, like someone accused of date rape.'[14] Equally typical was the comment of Senator Marian Bergeson, author of the same state's law designed to increase the penalties for rape. Explaining that the increased penalties did not apply to offences not involving the use or threat of force, the Senator stated: 'That excludes persons accused of date rape ... [and] spousal rape.'[15]

THE CASE FOR TAKING THE DATE OUT OF RAPE

Among the spousal rapes uncovered by Finkelhor and Yllo was one where a woman was jumped in the dark by her husband and forcibly buggered over a woodpile; one where a woman was raped by her husband immediately after returning home from hospital having had gynaecological surgery (he caused her to haemorrhage and she had to return to hospital as a result); one where a woman's husband ripped a six centimetre gash in her vagina in the course of 'trying to pull her vagina out'.[16] These are the spousal rapes which, according to common perceptions, are non-violent.

The trauma suffered by women who are date raped is no less than that experienced by those who are the victims of the more 'conventional' rape. On the day after Mike Tyson was released from prison into a dazzle of adoring fans and the world's press, the *Sunday Times* reported that Desiree Washington, his victim, 'has seen much of her personal life fall apart since she testified in 1992 against Tyson ... Her parents divorced due to the pressure of the publicity. The comfortable family home ... has been sold. Her younger sister was bullied at school by thugs who thought Washington "asked for it". Her mother lost her job ... and is now on a state disability pension due to depression and stress ... Washington's confident, outgoing personality has practically disappeared.' The paper linked Washington's trauma with the rape trial, rather than the rape itself.[17] But her story is similar to that of many rape victims, irrespective of whether their attackers were strangers or dates.

A survey carried for Channel 4 *Dispatches* found just as much violence in acquaintance rape cases as in stranger rapes. Among the women raped by lovers and ex-lovers, friends and work colleagues was one (raped at a friend's party) who was strangled and whose head was bashed against a wall until she passed out; a 17-year-old whose boyfriend hit her with a plank of wood before raping and buggering her; and a woman whose former partner threatened to kill her, tore off her clothes and held a scissors at her throat as he raped her.[18]

THE FORMS OF DENIAL IN THE MEDIA

As well as trivializing the effects of date rape on victims, many commentators also excuse the perpetrators. Typical of this attitude is Geoffrey Wheatcroft in the *Independent on Sunday*. Mike Tyson and Angus Diggle, Wheatcroft pronounced, were: 'victims of society... The shelves of suburban shops groan with skin mags and "adult" videos, schoolboys play pornographic computer games. Then they are expected to grow up like Boy Scouts, who never forget that every girl is another chap's sister.'[19] This approach is as disturbing as it is asinine. First, Wheatcroft relies on the ready availability of pornography to excuse men from responsibility for rape. In general, men are the creators, the consumers and the beneficiaries of pornography. That they should then be *excused* for abusive behaviour because of its existence is intolerable. Secondly Wheatcroft appears to assume that women are only to be respected by virtue of their relationships with other men, in this case their brothers. Not every woman is another 'chap's' sister. And even if we were, why shouldn't men respect us for *ourselves*?

As a crowning idiocy, on top of mocked victims and excused perpetrators, the media presents us with the real culprits in the whole affair – women themselves, and feminists in particular. Brian Appleyard complains that 'Sexual manners have been ripped out of the realm of local custom and culture and flung into the entirely inappropriate realm of politics and the law.' Forced sex becomes an issue of *manners*, like farting during intercourse, or indulging in a post-coital cigarette. And *feminism* rather than male violence, is blamed for a chilling in male-female relations. Appleyard goes on to complain that 'By identifying itself as a revolutionary force in people's intimate lives [feminism] has created an embittered climate in which crass generalizations about sexual behaviour are tending to crush the normal process of custom and traditional wisdom.'[20] Presumably, Appleyard is complaining that arguments about women's right to say no are, in his view, gaining sway over more sensible rules such as 'women who wear short skirts are asking for it.'

THE CASE FOR TAKING THE DATE OUT OF RAPE

And of course it isn't just 'feminists' who are blamed for 'date rape'. The individual women who are raped are also held responsible for their fates. David Thomas, for example, appears to adopt the old 'victim provocation' approach when he draws a spectacularly facile analogy between the rape of a 'sex kitten' and the mugging of someone who 'walked through the streets of the South Bronx carrying a placard which read "I carry gold Amex and Mastercard".'[21] And those women who are not being blamed for being sexually provocative are castigated for their communication failures. Utterly typical was this comment in the *Ottawa Citizen*: 'Women are afraid of being an inconvenience, of speaking their mind, of being assertive for fear of being labelled a "bitch" ... women must learn to speak up and voice their desires clearly and loudly.'[22]

Then, finally, many women are simply the wrong 'type'. So, for example, when William Kennedy Smith was accused of rape the *New York Times* reported with relish that his alleged victim: (a) had an illegitimate child – 'It's unclear why the couple did not marry'; (b) had committed 17 traffic offences; (c) went out to nightclubs where *she sometimes drank alcohol*; (d) when she was at school, had had friends who drove fast cars, went to parties and played truant. In addition, her mother had married above her station, and her school grades weren't great. The message seemed to be either that this (very average) history suggested that she was lying or, that even if she could be believed, she 'had it coming to her.'[23]

The Forms of Denial
in Society

'Hasn't the bitch already brought enough shame to this village?'
(*Observer Magazine*).[1] The 'bitch' was Bahveri Devi, a middle-aged
Indian woman from a village in Rajasthan. Her crime was to have
complained of gang-rape by several respectable (and higher-caste)
village men. Devi, a *sathin* (volunteer social worker) was one of many
women working to end child-marriage and the murder of baby girls,
both of which (although illegal) are common in the region. At the
time of the alleged rape she was trying to stop the marriage of a
young girl from one of the men's families. According to one journalist,
'The gang rape was clearly a ploy to teach the women of Bhateri and
neighbouring villages a lesson. It appears to have been devastatingly
effective. In an area where women had started speaking out against
sexual discrimination … they have been forbidden since the rape to
attend public meetings or speak to outsiders.'[2]

And what of Bahveri Devi? According to the same journalist,
she was left a 'broken woman, totally ostracised in her village' and

regarded as 'an immoral woman who cried rape to hide her own sins'. Another woman who had trained as a social worker in the same village told the *Observer* magazine, 'Rape is actually very common in Indian villages ... but because of the shame and stigma it goes largely unreported ... the victim knows that she will be labelled for life ... the stigma will be attached not only to her but also to her family and the village.' If we are to believe Bahveri Devi, she was punished first by being raped, and then again for complaining of it. Her failure to play the game correctly afterwards – her decision to go to the police, to complain of the rape, to refuse to remain silent – resulted in her being ostracized and denounced by her fellow villagers.

Bahveri Devi is alone in her Indian village, but she is not alone in her experience. Her story may represent an extreme example of the ill-treatment of women who complain of rape, but there are many other such stories. In April 1989 a woman was attacked, raped and sodomized and beaten half to death by a gang of youths in Central Park, New York. When the case came to trial in August of the following year, protesters lined the streets outside. As she arrived at the courthouse, the picketers screamed 'She's a prostitute, she's a whore!'. They were angry because the jogger was White and middle-class, her attackers Black.[3]

Although the vast majority of rapes involve attackers and victims of the same race, the public perception of the 'rapist' is frequently the product of racism. The myth of the Black rapist was particularly powerful in nineteenth-century America and Black men convicted of raping White women were far more severely punished than White rapists, or the Black rapists of Black women. Even prostitutes, if they were White, could sometimes see Black attackers convicted. In 1912 an Atlanta court declared: 'The consensus of public opinion, unrestricted to either race, is that a White woman prostitute is yet, though lost of virtue, above the even greater sacrifice of the voluntary submission of her person to the embraces of the other race.'[4]

THE FORMS OF DENIAL IN SOCIETY

Today, while the letter of the law does not discriminate between White and Black, whether as attackers or as victims of rape, in practice, the situation is rather different. In the United States, for example, Black women are considerably less likely to see their alleged attackers convicted of rape, and Black men who are convicted of rape receive considerably higher sentences than White men (at least when the victim is White).[5] Nor are there any prizes for guessing which type of rape generates the most lurid headlines. The *Independent on Sunday* pointed out that on the same night in April 1989 that the Central Park attack took place, 'There were seven murders and eight shootings in the city. A woman was shot in the back of the head, smashed with a cinder block, sexually abused with a five-inch length of pipe, and found under an elevated highway in the Bronx; it didn't make the front pages. She was not white or middle-class'.

To the extent that some convictions resulted, it is possible that the Central Park jogger may have benefitted from racism within the judicial system. But she never asked to be attacked and, by all accounts, would have suffered the same assault regardless of the colour of her skin. Her injuries were still apparent when she attended court. But all of this visible pain could not counteract, for those outside the courtroom, the assumption that she was an evil, lying whore who had brought it on herself and was motivated simply by racism.

And you don't have to be a White victim of rape to generate this kind of hatred. Desiree Washington was widely seen as a traitor to her people when she accused Mike Tyson of rape. According to Tyson's promoter, Don King, the Tyson episode 'was a "black-on-black crime", Tyson its victim'.[6] More recently Marc Cummings protested, in *Ethnic News Watch* that 'Our women have become useful figures in the demise of Black men ... politically, women being used to discredit Black men of prominence has become an effective tool for political manoeuvring ... The Mike Tyson rape trial is an example of how Black men can be used as political insurance. Tyson was the "sacrificial" lamb for the legitimacy of date rape.'[7]

The stories of Desiree Washington, Bahveri Devi and the Central Park jogger all show the hatred directed at women who complain of rape. Whatever their age and status, whatever the colour of their skin or the circumstances of the attack, no one is immune from allegations of spite. In 1977 a study of American adults found that over half of them believed that fifty per cent or more of rapes are reported as rape only because the woman was trying to get back at a man she was angry with or was trying to cover up an illegitimate pregnancy.[8] Another study revealed that 40 per cent of men thought that: 'In order to protect the male, it should be difficult to prove that a rape has occurred.'[9]

The disbelief doesn't just show up in statistics: it surfaces every time the subject of rape is discussed. So, for example, when Austen Donnellan was acquitted of rape, a fellow student told *The Times*: 'A friend of mine said if [Donnellan] is found guilty, it's going to give women who sleep with a guy they don't like the excuse to get them into trouble.'[10] And in the United States, college athletes complain about their vulnerability to false accusations. The *Denver Post* reported one college footballer saying: 'I remember when I was younger coming out of high school one of the first talks my dad had with me was "Watch out. When you're in a high-profile situation, some women will come to you and try to pin anything on you." Date rape, trying to say they're pregnant with your baby. That just frightens me to death.' What planet are these men on? Aren't there easier ways for women to have a go at men they don't like? Listening to this, one would be forgiven for thinking that men are so terrified of false allegations of rape that they have stopped having sex. Needless to say, of this there is little evidence.

The notion that women lie about rape is widely accepted in most cultures (and, as we shall see in the next chapter, shapes the approach of the legal system). But it's not the only idea that people have about rape. These ideas have been summarized as follows: 'Women mean "yes" when they say "no"; women are "asking for it" when they wear provocative clothes, go to bars alone, or simply walk down the street at night; only virgins can be raped; women are vengeful, bitter creatures "out to get men"; if a woman says "yes" once, there is no reason to believe her "no" the next time; women who "tease" men deserve to be raped; the majority of women who are raped are promiscuous or have bad reputations; a woman who goes to the home of a man on the first date implies she is willing to have sex; women cry rape to cover up an illegitimate pregnancy; a man is justified in forcing sex on a woman who makes him sexually excited; a man is entitled to sex if he buys a woman dinner; women derive pleasure from victimization.'[11]

These can be called rape myths, and they can be broken down into two categories: the denying of rape and the justifying of rape.

THE DENYING MYTHS

Some supposed motivations for false allegations of rape are so preposterous that they would be funny if it weren't for the fact that people actually believe them. In 1971, an American Professor of Psychiatry solemnly listed no less than thirty five reasons why women lie about rape.[12] These reasons included, together with the old standards such as pregnancy, revenge and venereal disease: child custody ('promiscuous wives, involved in divorce suits, sometimes make false claims of rape to protect their reputation'); loss of a boyfriend or husband ('young ladies who have lost the affection of a boyfriend may attempt to regain it by a dramatic appeal for sympathy'); the unwelcome stepfather (in order to get rid thereof); 'the first menstrual period' (?), and 'curfew violation'. In common with every other learned treatise on the reasons why women cry rape, the book provides no evidence that false complaints are anything but

rare. Instead of collecting hard information about the frequency
of lies, Professor MacDonald creates whole 'categories' of false
complaint from single instances where a complain *may* not have been
true (often simply where it was not believed), and from apocryphal
stories about girls getting pregnant or getting home late.

A decade later, Elliott (a British legal academic), proclaimed that
women have 'various and numerous causes for lying ... extrication
from difficulties caused by arriving home late, becoming pregnant,
contracting V.D., or being caught in the act of intercourse; feelings
of guilt about what was done in two minds and is now repented ...
getting one's own back at an unfaithful, or contemptuous, lover;
blackmail; confusion of fantasies with reality'. Finally he warns that:
'Alleged pack rape of a young complainant may be a consensual frolic
which has gone wrong only in that, for the first time, the girl failed to
reach home before her parents came home from work.'[13] Once more,
Elliott doesn't explain his suspicions by reference to actual cases,
much less statistics. His appeal is, it seems, to 'common sense'. The
idea that women make false allegations of rape is not confined to the
writings of professors of psychiatry and legal academics; it also plays
a role in the courtroom. In 1990 an English court freed a dentist who
had been accused of sexually assaulting no less than seven patients.
The sedative taken by the patients could, in the opinion of the judge,
have 'caused sexual fantasies'.[14] And in 1989, the English Court of
Appeal overturned an award of damages made by the High Court to
a teacher who claimed that she had been raped by a physiotherapist.
Lord Donaldson declared that the trial judge had allowed himself to
be carried away by 'his sympathy for the plaintiff, which all would
share regardless of whether she was the victim of actual or imaged
assaults of such gravity'. Great caution was needed in evaluating a
complaint of sexual assault, said Donaldson, and even greater caution
was required where the plaintiff had, as here, 'suffered a change of
personality and was suffering from an illness of an hysterical nature.'[15]

THE FORMS OF DENIAL IN SOCIETY

The unfortunate thing about this approach is that many women who have been raped do undergo 'personality changes' to the extent that being terrified about personal safety, having difficulty in trusting people, experiencing serious depression and, often, suicidal feelings, can be described as such. The medical profession is still quick to detect 'hysteria' in women, and what is seen as symptomatic of disorder may in fact be a rational response to an assault. To become less trusting, less open, may be an entirely sensible, if rather unfortunate, response. To counsel that extra caution be exercised in the cases of women who suffer 'change of personality' or 'illness of an hysterical nature' is perverse.

THE JUSTIFYING MYTHS[16]

The next category of myths regard rape as justifiable – they suggest that certain women deserve to be raped as a result of their behaviour or appearance. A woman may deserve rape because she has behaved in such a way as to signify consent to sexual intercourse (this may be by going to a man's apartment on a first date, by allowing him to buy her dinner, by asking him out, by wearing a low-cut dress or a short skirt). She may also earn rape by breaching some other standard of proper feminine behaviour (by getting drunk, for example).

These notions all rely on the bizarre view of sex as something women can tie themselves into in advance, after which time we are obliged to go through with it whether we want it or not. But how many people really think like this? Little statistical evidence exists about British attitudes, although anecdotal evidence abounds; in the United States, on the other hand, innumerable studies have been conducted amongst school children, college students and adults.

In 1979, 54 per cent of Californian male high-school students thought rape was justifiable if a female 'leads a boy on'. In 1980,

Jurors and Rape reported the results of a study conducted to assess the attitudes to rape of 1056 potential jurors. Sixty-six per cent of those interviewed thought that rape was provoked by the victims' behaviour or appearance; 34 per cent thought women should be responsible for preventing their own rapes; and 11 per cent thought that women who were raped were 'asking for it'. The authors pointed out that, if the findings could be extrapolated from these potential jurors to others, 'it would appear that rather substantial numbers of people attribute rape primarily to women, not to men'.[17]

It's OK to rape women who are drunk. A recent *Time*/CNN telephone survey of 500 Americans found that 17 per cent of men and 9 per cent of women thought that a man who had sex with a woman who was actually unconscious with drink or drugs should not be classified as rape. One newspaper report points out that 'Some prosecutors refuse to take acquaintance rape cases in which the alleged victim had been drinking, because juries typically conclude that such circumstances actually preclude the possibility of rape'.[18] It goes on to reveal that one third of adults aged 18–49 thought that 'a raped woman was "partly to blame" if she was under the influence of alcohol or drugs'. This rose to more than half of those aged over 50.

Let's get some perspective here. We are allowed to drink within a legal limit and drive; surely we should be allowed to drink and talk to men? It is true that a woman who has had something to drink may be less quick to spot a potential problem; this may mean that she is less likely to avert a potential rape. It doesn't mean she bears any responsibility for it; it's not her fault if she fails to predict what is going to happen, or if she can't run away fast enough. It's not my fault (whether or not I've just been in the pub) if I fail to jump out of the way of a speeding car which mounts the pavement and crushes me into a wall. Anyway, why should women be required to uphold the moral highground when it comes to alcohol. It isn't women who use drink as an excuse to rape people.

THE FORMS OF DENIAL IN SOCIETY

Just as rape can be justified by women's drinking, so it can be justified by their 'leading men on'. One review of the many studies conducted in the United States concluded that up to 50 per cent of men regard it as acceptable 'for a guy to hold a girl down and force her to have sexual intercourse' if, for example, 'she gets him sexually excited' or 'she says she's going to have sex with him and then changes her mind'.[19]

Judges as well as jurors share these views. One American judge recently informed researchers that: 'The typical rape case involves a tremendous amount of asking for it. The average rape is a girl, well-endowed ... went to a tavern, drank all night, expected a sexual encounter and got raped – he used more force than she expected ... I believe biologically it is wrong to entice a man knowing the situation you're creating and then saying "no". There is a button a man has that cannot be turned off and on like a light switch. And a man can go to prison for a very long time because of it'.[21]

Merely being sexually active is apparently also enough to justify rape. In 1990 Terry Hamblin (at the time a consultant haematologist in Bournemouth) declared that research findings which suggested a very high incidence of STDs in raped women 'add more credence to the frequent male excuse that "she was asking for it"'.[21] What exactly does Hamblin mean by 'asking for it'? In the first place, the study upon which he relied couldn't distinguish between pre-existing STDs and those present in the rapists' sperm, so it may have been the case that the rapists, rather than their victims, had an unusually high rate of disease. But even if the women had been infected prior to the rapes, how did he get from this to 'asking for it?' The professor is confusing sex with rape. Or could it be that Hamblin meant that it doesn't matter if sexually active women are raped; that women who behave like tarts may be treated as tarts; that it is unacceptable to refuse to Jack what has been willingly given to Tom, Dick and Harry?

Other types of justification focus on the notion that rape is what women really want. This view has been popular for many years. Originally it was supported on the basis that, since society forbade women from engaging in illicit sex, their protestations about sex functioned simply as a nod to convention and were not to be taken seriously. 'No' couldn't be relied upon to mean 'no'. Or, according to the recently departed Sir Nicholas Fairbairn: 'The understanding of words is everything in communication, except perhaps the eyes – and that is restricted to women who have the eyes to say "yes" and the tongue to say "no".'[22] One wonders how Sir Nicholas got to be such an expert on what women really want.

The no means yes approach operates on the assumption that women want sex but, for one reason or another, choose to be coy. At least such an attitude allows us the dignity of knowing what we want. But there is an approach which is even worse – the idea that women don't actually know what they want. On this approach a woman could think that she didn't want sex when, in fact, she did. And if a man had sex with her under these circumstances he shouldn't be convicted of rape because, although he ignored her 'no's, her struggles, and so on: although he may have forced her down, hit her and overpowered her, she was on one level (albeit subconsciously) consenting. And if she was consenting, it can't have been rape.

To allow men to decide what women really want is obviously quite mad. But this type of argument has exerted a massive influence – in particular, over the legal treatment of rape. It became fashionable, conveniently enough, just as society's straitjacket on women's sexual morality began gradually to loosen its hold. Just as women, gradually, began to be allowed to say yes to sex (with the result that their no's became more worthy of belief), Freudian analysis of women's sexuality replaced Victorian morality as the excuse for deafness to women's no's. Helen Deutsch developed the full-blown psychoanalyst's theory of rape. Masochism, to Deutsch, was 'the most elementary power in a woman's life'. Women, according to Deutsch, desire rape.[23] And if women desire rape, then surely they consent to it. The absurd notion that women crave rape has been discredited – even if some women do fantasize about it (and very few do[24]) there is a world of difference between fantasy and reality. But it continues to exert a profound influence on the treatment of women who complain of rape.

In one particularly awful twist, women also demonstrate that they really want it if they try to limit the injury involved in rape by asking their assailant to wear a condom. In Texas in 1992 a man had broken into the victim's home, held her at knife-point, and forced her to have sex. She asked him to use a condom because she was afraid of being infected with AIDS. She fled, naked, at the earliest opportunity. Consent was the only question at issue; a grand jury refused to try the case.[25]

Studies have consistently shown that men misinterpret women's behaviour as sexually inviting when it is not.[26] Even when undergraduates were shown videos which were meant to depict sexual harassment, 'Men perceived the female target as behaving in a "sexier" manner regardless of her status, the level of harassment, or the victim's response.' Most significantly for our purposes: 'Men's misperceptions persist regardless of whether the [woman] accepts or rejects the [man's] advances.'[27] This neatly illustrates quite how difficult we make it for women who are raped. Numerous studies have shown that men perceive women's behaviour simply in being women as 'sexual', even when the women give no indications of interest.

In addition to all of this, forced sex is justifiable if a man has earned the right to fuck a woman. A 1988 study of American teenagers found that one in four of the boys (and almost one-in-six girls) thought that forced sex was acceptable if a man had spent money on a woman (for example, by taking her out on a date). Sixty-five per cent of boys and 47 per cent of girls thought forced sex was acceptable if a man had been dating a woman for more than six months; and an amazing nine-out-of-ten boys and eight-out-of-ten girls if the man and woman were married.[28]

Sometimes rape is excused on the grounds that, while it is generally wrong, some mitigation operated in this particular case. The mitigator is usually to be found in the man's loss of sexual control. This idea depends on the assumption that rape is a sex-driven crime. In fact it is nothing of the sort. Diane Scully's research into convicted rapists, for example, indicated that few were sexually frustrated at the time of their rapes. Forty-six per cent of the rapists were married or cohabiting at the time and, while many of them physically abused the women they lived with they were, nevertheless, generally satisfied with their relationships. If it was sex they wanted, they could have had it at home.[29]

Scully also found that these men tended to place women on pedestals, in the sense of expecting unrealistically high standards of behaviour from them. When women failed to live up to these standards, the men felt entitled to rape and otherwise abuse them. The men Scully studied did talk in terms of being provoked, led on, drunk and so on. But, she says, they used these excuses and justifications for rape in order to represent their actions as acceptable.

The decision to rape was generally a conscious and deliberate one, which was afterwards explained in line with the common stereotypes. Men might, for example, claim that their victims had been provocatively dressed, but this didn't mean that the men had lost control. It meant, rather, that the women's clothing allowed the men to give themselves permission to rape them – after all, provocatively dressed women are 'asking for it'. The acceptance of rape myths such as this is, in fact a 'necessary precondition' for rape – in Scully's words: 'An important part of learning to rape includes the mastery of a vocabulary that can be used to explain sexual violence against women in socially acceptable terms.'[30]

THE FORMS OF DENIAL IN SOCIETY

Eighty of the 114 men interviewed by Scully admitted sexual contact with their victims. Thirty-three of these men denied rape (they accepted that sex had occurred but claimed that it wasn't rape). The other 47 admitted rape, although they tried to lessen the extent to which they should be blamed (and 'systematically' underestimated the degree of force they used).[31] Both groups used the rape myths we have been considering to justify or excuse their actions. So, for example, 25 per cent of those men who denied rape claimed that the woman had made sexual advances to them, and a further 17 per cent claimed that she had been seductively dressed. Others claimed that no meant yes, or simply refused to accept that forced sex with a woman who had violated traditional standards of feminine behaviour (by, for example, being alone in a bar or accepting a lift from someone met casually), constituted rape.

Rapists who knew their victims were more likely than others to deny that they were guilty of rape. So, too, were those whose victims had been hitchhiking or otherwise 'misbehaving' when they were attacked. Most interesting, however, is the fact that rapists who denied their guilt actually reinvented the details of their rapes in order to bring the rape myths into play.

Scully's findings paint a very similar picture of those of studies carried out on unconvicted, self-disclosed rapists. These men, like those imprisoned for rape, rape because they think it's OK. One study of men who admitted having used force to obtain sex found that, while two thirds of them accepted that their behaviour fitted the legal definition of rape, they claimed that their victims' behaviour entirely absolved them from blame.[32] These men accepted the rape myths.

The Forms of Denial
in the Legal System

We have considered the way that rape has been treated throughout history, and the way in which it is commonly thought of today. This chapter sets out to explore how the legal system reacts to women who complain of rape. I will consider both the law itself (the way in which rape is defined) and how it operates in practice (police decision-making, court practice, and so on), and will look at the US and Canada as well as the UK. The picture which will emerge is a familiar one. Just as history has been selective about the types of forced sex which were treated as rape; just as, culturally, we accept many episodes of forced sex as normal; so too, legal systems are very particular about which incidents of forced sex they accept as rape.

The definition of rape I will use here is conservative. What I mean by rape is sex to which a woman does not consent when the man knows that she is not or may not be consenting, or couldn't care less whether she is consenting or not. This definition of rape is just that which is laid down by English law (Sexual Offences Act 1976, s.1).

Rape is defined as sex without consent and, in order to be guilty, the man must have been at least reckless as to the woman's lack of consent. Recklessness includes awareness of a risk and the 'couldn't care less' attitude of my definition. English law, in addition, provides that the (sober) man who genuinely believes that the woman is consenting to sex is not guilty of rape no matter how absurd, arrogant or unreasonable that mistake is. While this is not an approach which I would embrace, I shall accept it for the purposes of this chapter.

What is striking about this definition of rape is that it appears to cover all types of rape. Far from applying only to the ideal model of rape we have been discussing, this definition demands no injury, applies regardless of whether the man is a stranger or a lover, and contains no requirement that the women is respectable, much less a virgin. The definition even applies, since 1995, if a man rather than a woman is the victim of the attack.

The English definition of rape applies in Wales. In Scotland the sex has to take place against the woman's will, rather than without her consent, but this makes little practical difference.[1] In the US the law differs from state to state. In some states men cannot be found guilty of raping their wives. Other states have abolished this exception while others yet have actually extended it to cover co-habitees and, worse, to provide a partial defence of 'voluntary social companionship'. This approach, suggested by the influential Model Penal Code (and followed by a number of states) grades rape as a less serious offence if the woman was either voluntarily in the company of the man at the time of the rape or, at any time in the past, had 'permitted him sexual liberties'.[2]

Some US states define rape widely to include forced anal and oral sex, as well as the penetration of anus or vagina by objects or parts of the body other than the penis. In these states, women as well as men can be convicted of rape and men, as well as women, can be victims of the offence. Some US states have done away entirely with the crime of 'rape' (as has Canada), and replaced it with a ladder of offences, which are graded in terms of seriousness, and carry maximum penalties ranging from ten years to life. In these jurisdictions, the offences are typically defined as increasingly serious according to the degree of force used and injury inflicted on the victim.

What is common to just about all definitions of rape is that sex must take place without the consent of the victim. In England and Wales this is explicit in the legislation. In most US states it is not, rape being defined instead in terms of the man's use or threat of 'force' or 'forcible compulsion'. Even in those US states where a lack of consent is not explicitly demanded by the legislation, consent still operates as a defence to rape so, in practice, lack of consent is part of the offence.[3] The requirement that force is used or threatened is additional to the requirement that the woman did not consent. This makes the typical US definition of rape narrower than those in the UK. In practice, however, in the UK a woman will be seen as having consented to sex unless the defendant used or threatened force. As a result, the definitions of rape which operate in the UK and those which operate in various American states are not dissimilar. They will be discussed in detail later.

RAPE AND THE LAW IN THEORY

On the surface, rape law seems to treat victims of the offence with fairness. Women do not have to struggle to the point of serious injury in order to be found not to have consented to sex and, in the US at least, a man who unreasonably decides that a woman is consenting when she is not, can be convicted of rape. It seems, if anything, that women have a better deal than men. In most jurisdictions only men can be prosecuted for rape, and in many only women can be the victims of the offence. Not only are women more likely to be protected by rape laws than are men, but taxpayers' money is spent on providing rape suites where women who complain of rape can be examined in comfort, and on specialist training for police officers who interview them. No other crime victims (except, perhaps, sexually abused children) are given such special treatment.

On top of this, women who come forward to complain of rape are generally not named by the press. In the UK, specific laws require that their privacy is respected (in Scotland they even get to testify in a courtroom closed to the public). While only a few US states have such laws (and even these appear to be incompatible with the US constitution and therefore unenforceable), the US media generally respect women's privacy and do not publish their names. (The Florida *Globe*'s naming of the woman who accused William Kennedy Smith of rape was condemned even by much of the US media.[4]) Finally, special rape shield laws exist in the UK, American states, Australia and Canada, which protect women from having details of their sexual histories used in court cases.

When rapists are convicted they are often given very heavy penalties indeed. The life sentence is available in the UK for those convicted of rape and, both here and elsewhere, is sometimes used. In 1993, for example, a man known to the press as the 'Beast of Barking' received two life-sentences when he was convicted of raping and buggering one girl, and committing two indecent assaults on other women. The following year another man received eighteen life-sentences for a series of attacks on young girls over a fifteen-year period. These sentences are even more striking when they are compared with the five-year sentences often passed on people convicted of manslaughter.

And England is not the only place where rapists are treated harshly. In 1994, Florida's State Senate voted to castrate twice-convicted rapists and to impose the death sentence on men who offended three times (but whose first two offences, presumably, pre-dated the castration law). In the same year, California passed a 'one-strike' law designed to imprison rapists for life after only one conviction (other offenders get at least three 'strikes'), and the longest sentence ever passed in Minnesota (139 and two thirds years) was received by Timothy Baugh. He had been convicted of fourteen sexual assaults carried out over a period of eighteen months.[5]

RAPE AND THE LAW IN PRACTICE

But there is a yawning gap between theory and practice. For all the public uproar, the political posturing and the swingeing sentences inflicted on a few, conviction rates for rape remain appallingly low, and many women who do complain report a 'second rape' at the hands of the legal system. Fear of this second assault has been shown to contribute to women's extreme reluctance to report rape (it is widely estimated, both in the UK and in the US and Canada, that only about one in ten attacks are ever reported). Of those women who do go to the police, barely one in ten of these will see their attackers convicted. Many more will not even have their complaints acknowledged by the police.

The US Federal Bureau of Investigation estimated, in 1991, that complaints of rape were four times as likely to be dismissed by the police as were other serious crimes. Some years previously a survey of police officers across the US showed that some officers believed that as many as 96 per cent of all rape complaints were untrue.[6] In the UK studies suggest that almost half of all complaints of rape and attempted rape are not recorded by the police as crimes.[7] This seems to have remained constant since the early 1980s, despite Home Office guidelines issued in 1986, which were intended to increase the recording rate. (The guidelines require that all complaints of rape and serious sexual assault should be recorded unless the woman withdraws the allegation and accepts that it had been false). While the police are likely to be much more sympathetic to complainants than they were ten years ago, and while women are more likely to be interviewed in comfortable rape suites than in chilly interview rooms, it seems that they are just as unlikely to see anything actually done about their complaints.[8]

Even if a rape complaint is recorded by the police, this is only the first step. In the US and Britain, the police investigate recorded complaints and, if they identify and trace a suspect or suspects, then decide whether or not to proceed with the case. If they decide to do so they pass the matter over to the prosecuting authority. It is then for the prosecutor to decide whether charges should be pressed and, if so, what the charges should be. The prosecutor could, for example, decide to press less serious charges (manslaughter instead of murder, indecent assault instead of rape or attempted rape) in return for a guilty plea from the defendant. He or she could equally decide to drop the case entirely on the basis that a jury is unlikely to convict.

How are rape complaints dealt with by the prosecuting authorities? It is very difficult to find an answer in England and Wales, since the Crown Prosecution Service does not keep records of decisions categorized according to particular offences. A 1988–90 London study, however, found that the CPS went ahead with only 80 per cent of rape/attempted rape cases referred to them by the police (which, in turn, amounted to only 30 per cent of the reported offences).[9] And things are getting worse. In 1993, three times as many rape cases were dropped by the CPS after the initial court appearance as had been dropped in 1985.[10] In the US, figures vary from state to state, but it is clear that there is a higher rate of 'no-proceedings' decisions in rape complaints than in other crimes.[11]

And what of the lucky few who manage to get their complaints as far as the courtroom? Not only will many of them find that their attackers are acquitted, but they themselves will have undergone the most extreme form of public humiliation. Women who complain of rape in the UK will have been questioned in front of a room full of strangers about their sexual behaviour, their use of contraception and their taste in underwear. Any history of contraceptive use, abortion or psychological problems (depression, childhood eating disorders and so on) will have been made available to defence barristers; they may use it pretty much as they please.

Women will have had to stand in the witness box while the underwear they wore at the time of the attack is passed around the jurors by a court official. They will have been painted by defence lawyers as tawdry and undiscriminatingly promiscuous. It will have been suggested, regardless of the truth, that their allegations are the result of jealousy or spite. Having been subjected to this ordeal, many women will find that their attackers walk free.

According to Mariette Smith, senior co-ordinator at one of London's victim support centres: 'The whole thing breaks down when [women] go to court. They are treated like rubbish ... I think in court things are getting worse ... They bring everything in these days ... They will go into every aspect of a woman's life.' Smith told of one case in which the defence called the Family Planning Association 'to give evidence on whether it was necessary for a young woman to have a large number of condoms with her ... the woman had been handcuffed during rape'.[12]

EXPLAINING THE GAP: 'IDEAL' RAPE

Why this gulf between theory and practice? Closer examination of the recording, prosecution and conviction rates show that the treatment of rape complainants depends on much more than simply whether their alleged attacks fit the legal definition of rape.

The rape complainant's first contact within the legal system is the police, who record and investigate alleged crimes, interview and, if necessary, arrest suspects and pass cases on to the prosecuting authorities for further action. Numerous studies of the police have shown that officers are incredibly sceptical about rape complaints. One Scottish study found that police officers assumed that many complaints of rape were false. Fairly typical was a detective inspector who claimed that only three of the thirty or forty rape complainants he had come across in twenty years of police work had been genuine victims of the offence. When actually asked about false complaints, by contrast, officers could recall only one or two such cases.[13] Another study in London in 1988–1990, also found that high levels of scepticism remained. Despite the fact that the police 'operated under a clear instruction that no one reporting a sexual assault is to be disbelieved', that complainants were assigned specially trained women officers, and that 'at one level, the police officers seemed committed to making the new policies work', the researchers still found that 'old attitudes die hard'. Many officers thought that false allegations of rape were a common occurrence, citing apocryphal stories about women accusing their boyfriends after arguments, unpaid prostitutes accusing their clients, girls making up stories to explain unwanted pregnancies or late arrivals home. One police inspector claimed that 50 per cent of reported rapes were probably lies. Naturally, he was unable to provide any evidence in support of this.[14]

But the police are not sceptical about *all* rape reports. In Scotland, the complaints they really distrusted were those made by women who knew their attackers, or who had previously had sexual relationships with them, or who had simply been out socially (and drinking) when they were attacked.[15] Another 1985 study showed that police were much more likely to record complaints if they involved rapes 'committed by strangers; if additional violence and weapons were used; if the victim suffered additional injuries; if there had been no contact of a social nature between the victim and the offender immediately prior to the offence'.[16] And in the US, police action depends upon officers' perceptions of victims' 'misconduct' (which includes drinking and hitchhiking); their reputations, ages and occupations; and upon the relationship between accuser and accused.[17] A Philadelphia study found that 'poor women, women of color, prostitutes and those dependent on alcohol or drugs' are more likely to have their cases ignored by the police. Overweight women also encounter prejudice and hostility; police in Philadelphia did not believe obese women when they reported being raped.[18]

The police are not alone in disbelieving women who complain of rape. US research shows that prosecutors' decisions are also determined, in part, by the extent of physical injury sustained by the complainant; the level of force used by the alleged attacker; the existence of any previous relationship between them; and the woman's sexual history. Prosecutors were much more ready to use lie-detectors on rape complainants than on witnesses complaining of other crimes, and did so 'in order to ferret out cases where the girl is getting revenge or just bad'.[19] In Britain the collapse of a number of recent high-profile date-rape cases has caused some newspapers to complain that the Crown Prosecution Service is over eager to press charges in non-traditional cases, particularly in respect of allegations of date rape. But the latest available research suggests that rape complaints are in fact still less likely to be pursued by the CPS where the alleged victim is not a stranger to the accused.[20]

Even if a non-traditional rape complaint actually gets as far as court, the woman's difficulties are not over. Studies have consistently shown that the result in court depends on all the same factors again. Zsuzannah Adler carried out a major study of rape cases tried in England's central criminal court (the Old Bailey) in the early 1980s. She found that the chances of conviction depended closely on the extent to which the alleged rape matched the pattern of the ideal rape. Not a single case which lacked all of the attributes of the 'ideal rape' (i.e. 'where the victim is sexually inexperienced and has a "respectable" lifestyle, whose assailant is a stranger and whose company she had not willingly found herself in. She will have

THE FORMS OF DENIAL IN THE LEGAL SYSTEM

fought back, been physically hurt and, afterwards, promptly reported the offence') resulted in conviction.[21] More recently, a 1988–90 study found that three out of four trials where a stranger was accused of rape or attempted rape, but only two in ten of those in which the alleged attacker was known to the complainant, resulted in convictions. So serious was the disparity between the rapes reported to the police and those resulting in convictions that the researchers concluded: 'More women are coming forward, and on the whole, are now being treated with greater sensitivity by the police [than in 1985]. At the same time, the possibility of gaining a conviction appears from our data to have diminished.'[22]

Why are these factors, even when they are not part of the legal definition, so important to the outcome of a rape complaint? It is obvious that attacks which result in serious physical injury are easier to prosecute than those which do not – questions such as whether the woman consented tend to be easier to settle. It is also understandable that notions of victim responsibility will have an effect – human nature is such that we can escape some of the horror of violent crime by shifting the blame onto the victim. If we do this we can persuade ourselves that the same is unlikely to happen to us – if Jane got raped because she was a slut then, by behaving respectably (or by ensuring that our daughters do), we can avoid a similar fate.

This is all very well, but it does not explain fully the level of reluctance which society displays when it comes to dealing with non-ideal rape allegations. Many such allegations do involve physical injury or other evidence of forced sex. And as far as victim-blaming is concerned, people wearing a great deal of flashy gold jewellery may be ticked off when they are mugged, but we still punish the muggers.

It is in the courtroom itself that we have to look for an explanation of the gap between theory and practice. What happens in a rape trial? The first thing to remember is that the woman is only a witness to the crime. In criminal cases there are two 'parties', the *state* and the defendant (who is accused of the crime). The victim's role is taken over by the state, and the victim acts only (if at all) as a witness to the defendant's wrongdoing. The lawyers who do battle in court are those representing the state (the prosecution) and the accused (the defence). The victim, unlike the accused, does not have a lawyer. In Britain she will have been interviewed by a prosecution solicitor before the trial, but will not have spoken to the prosecution barrister who actually appears in court. While the accused will have discussed his case with his barrister before the trial, the complainant is not allowed to discuss the case with the prosecution barrister before the trial. When she stands up in court to give evidence, therefore, she does not know what to expect. There is no lawyer whose job it is to look after *her*. Her conflict with the defendant has been taken over by the state, but she has no say in what happens, no role except to answer the questions put to her. When the woman takes the stand in court, she will first be questioned by the prosecution barrister, who will ask her about the alleged attack. The defence barrister will then cross-examine her in order to try to shake her story, to root out any inconsistencies and to question her about aspects of her personal history that might make her story less worthy of belief.

It is not until the prosecution has introduced all its witnesses (there may be medical evidence from a police doctor, as well as statements from the police officers who originally interviewed the woman together with anyone who saw or heard anything which might be useful to the prosecution), that the defence has to bring forward its own witnesses. If the prosecution's case is very weak the judge may decide to dismiss the case at 'half-time' – before the defence have introduced their own witnesses (including the defendant). More commonly, the defence are asked to put their case before the judge sums up the main factual and legal arguments and the jury is asked to consider their verdict. They should only find the defendant guilty if they are *sure* (beyond any reasonable doubt) that he is guilty of the

THE FORMS OF DENIAL IN THE LEGAL SYSTEM

offence as charged. If they think that there is any real chance that he is not guilty, they should acquit him.

The set-up in court for a rape complainant is no different than for a householder who alleges that his house has been burgled, or a store detective who claims to have caught the defendant shoplifting. But someone accused of burglary may well have left their footprints on the flowerbed or their fingerprints on the windowsill. They may have been caught with the stolen property, or trying to get rid of it. The householder will generally be able to point to a broken window or other evidence of uninvited entry, and no one will seriously suggest that he was 'asking' to be burgled. Equally, where the eager store detective has collared a light-fingered shopper, they will generally have taken the suspect to the manager's office where, in the presence of several people, the suspect will have been asked to empty his pockets or his shopping basket.

The problem for the rape complainant is that she will not usually have witnesses to her story. Rapists are not generally known for striking in daylight in busy shopping centres. If women are attacked on the street it will usually be at night, and their attacker(s) will drag them into alleyways in order to complete the assault. More commonly, when women are attacked indoors (as they usually are), the best they can hope for is that a downstairs neighbour hears thudding on the floor, or the sound of a struggle. Even if this does happen, however, such noises don't necessarily mean anything about consent.

Advances in science make it increasingly easy to pin an attack on the man responsible (even if he wears a condom, his victim may have some of his skin under her nails, or his hair or saliva on her body). But no scientific method can ascertain whether consent was given or not. The best evidence that sex was not consented to will consist in physical injuries sustained by the woman and her alleged attacker. But women who are raped are often frightened, beyond all else, that they might be killed by their attackers; the police usually advise that resistance is unwise, at least where there is no clear path of escape. Herein lies the problem.

CORROBORATION

This difficulty of proving non-consent is unavoidable. But the law adds to the hurdles for women who are raped in a way it does not for other crimes. Until 1995 judges were required, in England and Wales, to warn juries about the evidence given by a woman who complained of rape. The judge had to warn the jury that it would be dangerous to rely on her word alone. This is called the 'corroboration warning' and, if it was not given and the defendant was convicted, his conviction would be reversed by the higher courts.

The requirement for the warning was removed by the Criminal Justice and Public Order Act 1994. But removing the requirement does not ban the practice. In Canada, after the mandatory warning was abolished in 1976, so many judges continued to issue it anyway that the government had to act again in 1982 to ban the warning entirely. And in Australia, its abolition in the early 1980s has not prevented judicial warnings since. One extraordinary example was provided by Judge Bollen of the South Australian Supreme Court. More than seven years after the abolition he related a yarn about a 'respectable businessman' accosted on a train by a 'respectably dressed woman' who, having torn her own clothes and inflicted injuries upon herself, cried 'rape'. 'So you can see', went on Judge Bollen, 'how careful we have to be about false allegations of rape.'[23]

Bollen's warning provides an example of the longevity of rape myths. Edwards discusses a false-accusation panic which occurred in Britain in the last thirty years of the nineteenth century. With the expansion of rail travel, 'a rapid succession of sex offence charges' were alleged against 'respectable' men by women who claimed to have been assaulted in railway carriages. The complaints may very well have been true. But, as Edwards points out, 'the legal process preferred to define [the accused men] as poor unsuspecting innocent gentlemen'; the women who complained were defined as 'vile conspirators and blackmailers', 'errant maids falsely accusing lovers to shelter themselves'.[24] Complaints of sexual assaults in railway carriages were automatically assumed to be false, and the myth of the railway accuser was born. As we have seen, the myth was to resurface in Australia a century later.

Some of the warnings which English judges have actually given to juries include the following: 'It is well known that women in particular and small boys are liable to be untruthful and invent stories'; 'This is a sex case. Experience has shown that women can and do tell lies for some reason, some for no reason at all'; 'It is well known that in sex cases women sometimes imagine things which various ingredients in their make-up tend to make them imagine.'

The requirement for a warning was almost unique to sexual offence trials, and suggested that complaints of sexual offences were much more likely to be false than were complaints of other crimes. But there is no truth in any such claim. Studies carried out by the police in Portland Oregon (1990) and in New York (1972) showed that the rate of false complaints of rape was 1.6 per cent and 2 per cent respectively, the same, if not lower, than that for other crimes.[25]

CREDIBILITY

All trials depend, to a certain extent, upon the perceived trustworthiness of the witnesses who give evidence to the court. A witness who is a convicted criminal, a renowned liar, or a notorious drunk is less likely to be believed than one who is known as a pillar of the local church and community. But the more central the witness' story is to the defendant's guilt, the closer the examination of his or her trustworthiness will be. It is unavoidable, as a result, that the rape complainant will be closely scrutinized by the jury. Since the defendant's conviction will often depend upon her word alone, it is crucial that that word is shown to be worthy of belief.

It is hardly surprising that the chances of a man being convicted of rape will fluctuate according to whether his alleged victim is a convicted fraudster or a well-known liar. What is not so obvious, however, is why those chances also depend upon whether she was a virgin prior to the alleged attack; whether she had an illegitimate child, or had ever had an abortion; whether she was on the pill; whether she slept with her boyfriend or not. But these issues are meat and drink to defence lawyers, and study after study has shown that any evidence (or suggestion) that a woman was sexually active (except in the context of marriage) practically guarantees a defendant's acquittal.

It is not clear (because they cannot be questioned in the UK about their verdicts) whether juries think that sexually active women are liars because they are sexually active; or that sexually active women consent indiscriminately to all sex and, therefore, must be lying when they claim to have been raped on any particular occasion; or that assaults on sexually active women are simply not serious enough to be punished as rape. Research in Canada has shown that 'any information at all implying that the victim had a prior sex history had the effect of reducing the perceived guilt of the accused regardless of whether this information was verified'.[26] In the US too, while neither the use of a weapon by the defendant nor physical injuries to the victim had much impact on jury verdicts; 'Jurors were influenced by a victim's "character". They were less likely to believe in a defendant's guilt when the victim had reportedly engaged in sex outside marriage, drank or used drugs, or had been acquainted with the defendant – however briefly – prior to the alleged assault.'[27]

The absurd notion that a woman's trustworthiness depends upon the number of men she has had sex with is not merely something that jurors have come up with by themselves. The reason why they have access to this information and why, as a result, they can continue to make decisions on the basis of it, is because the law has traditionally accepted the existence of a link between women's chastity and their truthfulness. Because sexual behaviour was traditionally frowned upon in women, sexually active women were seen as seriously immoral and, as a result, not to be trusted in anything. Time does not stand still, and even the law changes, however slowly, to reflect developing social attitudes. Over the last twenty years or so, England and Wales, Scotland, Canada and most Australian and US states have enacted 'rape shield' statutes. These laws usually declare that evidence of women's sexual activity is not to be admitted into the court for the purposes of deciding whether or not they are to be believed. But old habits die hard, and such is the conviction of many of those who apply the law that a woman's sexual behaviour simply must be relevant to whether or not the defendant is guilty of rape, that the judiciary in the various legal systems have carved exceptions to the different exclusionary rules.

English judges, for example, have reversed the legal rule (*see* page 84) that a woman's sexual history was not relevant to establish whether or not she consented to sex with the defendant. Evidence concerning women's sexual behaviour was welcomed back wholesale into rape trials. Things have got even worse recently because of a new rule (imposed in the wake of the scandalous miscarriages of justice in cases such as the Birmingham Six, the Guildford Four and Judith Ward) that prosecutors must disclose all their evidence to defence lawyers. Where this rule is applied to rape cases, defence lawyers get access to information about the woman's lifestyle and use of contraception.

In another legal rule unique to rape cases, women's reputations can be attacked by the accused man's lawyer without leaving him open to attack in turn. In all other cases, if a defendant attacks the character of the prosecution witnesses, he loses the shield that otherwise prevents jurors from being told about any of his past convictions. In rape, however, this rule does not apply, and the defence is therefore encouraged to proceed by slinging mud at the complainant and hoping that some sticks.

As for the other legal systems, even in those American states which laid down the most rigorous rules on the admission of sexual history evidence, it seems that such evidence continues to be introduced in court. In Michigan, for example, where a blanket ban was established as long ago as 1975, court officials still took the view (in the 1990s) that evidence that a rape complainant had indulged in casual sex would be admitted in court. Such evidence is entirely excluded by the rape shield statute. One Detroit judge was quoted as saying: 'It is only when a date rape misunderstanding occurs that, I think, the defendant couldn't get a fair trial without information about prior sexual conduct.'[28] This judge assumes that date rape is about 'misunderstanding'. Why should evidence that Jane had sex with three men in a four-month period be any more relevant to whether Barry raped her at home than it would be to whether Billy attacked her in an alleyway at night? In any case, the quotation serves to illustrate that, after fifteen years of the most radical rape legislation, the power of tradition still prevails amongst lawyers in Michigan as it does here in Britain. In Canada, too, where there are very strict rules regulating the circumstances in which a woman's sexual history evidence could be used in rape trials, the judges of the Supreme Court ruled, in 1991, that such evidence could be relevant to whether a woman had been raped.[29] So much for progress.

CONSENT

Perhaps the most difficult hurdle which women who complain of rape have to overcome is the tendency of judges and juries to presume consent from particular types of relationship and circumstances. The farther the facts stray from the frenzied attack by a mad stranger in the street, the more difficult it is to convince the jury that the woman did not consent to sex.

The defence of consent is always available to a man accused of rape. But in practice, when a man is charged with raping a total stranger who was not voluntarily in his company at the time, his lawyers argue not that the woman consented but, rather, that he was not the man who attacked her. The consent defence is the true ally of the man accused of raping his girlfriend, his date or the woman to whom he gave a lift home after a party. It is when rape is alleged in these sorts of circumstances that everything turns on consent and, in order to back up their clients' stories, defence lawyers will go fishing for any evidence of 'promiscuity' on the part of the woman concerned.

In England and Wales the rape shield law passed in 1976 aimed to prevent this kind of evidence being introduced in court. The judiciary, however, take a different view. Many rape convictions have been overturned on the basis that juries were not told about the complainant's sexual activities (activities which the appeal judges thought were relevant to whether she consented to sex with the defendant). In one case, evidence that a woman allowed a man to stay in her flat some weeks after the defendant allegedly raped her was accepted as relevant to whether she consented to sex with the defendant.[30] In another, evidence that a 14-year-old girl may not have been a virgin was considered relevant to whether she consented.[31] Such evidence is much more likely to be introduced in cases where the defendant and the complainant knew each other before the alleged attack. A survey for Channel 4's *Dispatches* (broadcast in early 1994) found that evidence of the woman's sexual history was used in 70 per cent of trials where rape by a non-stranger was alleged.

Even in those US states which have the strictest rape shield statutes, some commentators suggest that evidence of women's sexual history is still explored, 'as a matter of course'.[32] In contrast,

THE CASE FOR TAKING THE DATE OUT OF RAPE

if a woman's attacker has been accused of rape by someone else, even if he has been convicted of another attack, this cannot be brought to the attention of the jury. This rule appears to be enforced regardless of how similar the details of the different attacks alleged or proven.[33] So, for example, the jury in the William Kennedy Smith trial were never told that three other women had accused Smith of very similar assaults. According to the Palm Beach prosecutor, the common storyline to all four rape allegations was: 'Smith meets an attractive brunette at a party or similar gathering. He's the perfect gentleman. Then he gets her alone in his house or at a family home. He's still the perfect gentleman, until, without warning, something snaps, and he pounces, literally.'[34]

LOOKING BEHIND THE SPECIAL RULES

The argument generally put forward in response to those who complain of the way in which rape complaints are handled by the legal system is that caution and balance are needed to protect innocent men. But we will find that the rules are based, not on reason and logic but, instead, on assumptions about women, men and sex.

WOMEN ARE LIARS

In 1994 the corroboration rule was defended on the basis that 'allegations of sexual complaint are in many ways ones which are easily made ... and which, at the end of the day, are sometimes very difficult to refute'.[35] No evidence is *ever* produced for this oft-repeated statement. Each time the allegation is made it echoes only past declarations of the same unsupported prejudice. Women are far more likely to lie by denying rapes that have happened than inventing rapes that haven't.

The belief that women falsely accuse men of rape is also deeply ingrained into legal systems all over the world, and is responsible for other rules besides those relating to corroboration. In the United

States, for example, the influential Model Penal Code (upon which states base some or all of their criminal laws) suggests that women who do not complain about rape within three months of the alleged incident should be barred from complaining thereafter. The Code, which was completed and published as recently as 1980, explains that the time-bar is necessary not only to protect men from false accusations resulting from unwanted pregnancies or bitterness at relationships gone sour, but also to limit women's opportunities for blackmail.

WOMEN FIGHT 'REAL' RAPE

Does 'real' rape leave marks? Judge David Wild, summing up in a rape trial in Cambridge Crown Court in 1982 certainly thought that it did: 'If she doesn't want it,' the judge claimed, 'she only has to keep her legs shut and she would not get it without force and there would be marks of force being used'.[36]

It is true that a woman could resist rape to the point of injury. If we thought our 'chastity' more valuable than our lives then, perhaps, there would be fewer victims of rape. There might well, on the other hand, be rather more victims of murder. But surely we ought to have moved beyond the days when *The New York Times* praised Minnie Rauhauser (aged 17) for fighting 'bravely in defense of her honor'. Minnie fought off William Miller, who was trying to rape her. She managed, it seems, to prevent the rape. Instead he cut her throat 'from ear to ear'.[37] That was in 1891. Since then we have seen the sexual revolution, the decreasing importance of virginity for women and our significant strides towards being recognized as people rather than property. Surely it is time to recognize that women should not be expected to resist rape any more than we are expected to resist mugging, burglary or assault. Surely it is time to recognize that it is a better thing to be alive, and the victim of rape, than it is to be dead and 'undefiled'.

THE CASE FOR TAKING THE DATE OUT OF RAPE

At the heart of the problem is the law's understanding of women as sexually passive. In England and Wales, for example, the law which forbids incest makes it a crime for a man 'to have intercourse' with particular family members. For women, however, the crime is one of 'permitting' the relevant family members 'to have intercourse with her'.[38] The sexually passive woman is not confined to the law of incest either. Rape itself is defined as a man 'having intercourse' with a woman who does not consent. The word 'intercourse' suggests mutuality – social intercourse requires more than one person. But it seems that sexual intercourse requires a man and a receptacle.

If women aren't expected to participate in sexual intercourse, what is there to distinguish intercourse from rape? Passivity won't do, since this is accepted as an ingredient of normal sex, so action is required from the woman. Wouldn't a no suffice? Clearly not, as the law continues to see women as expected to say no whether they mean it or not. In order to distinguish rape from sex, therefore, that woman has to fight like a tiger. And even this, as we have seen, may not be enough.

MEN WHO RAPE ARE MONSTERS

The picture of rape as a crime which leaves its victims visibly and horribly wounded, and in which the absence of consent is unquestionable, depends in part on the notion of rapist as monster. One recent example of this can be found in the Dr Moffat's testimony in the Donnellan case: Robin Moffat, a senior forensic doctor with the Metropolitan police, testified that rapists were 'violent men', not 'kind, gentle and reliable like this defendant'.[39] Another example is the Court of Appeal's decision to quash the conviction of Peter Anderson. The Police officer had been jailed for seven years for raping 'a black, single mother' to whom he gave a lift home after a disco.[40] The Court of Appeal freed him because the judge had neglected to tell

the jury that he had no prior convictions. Respectable men
don't commit rape.

Rapists are painted as 'other' by the press – as serial attackers, loners, outsiders. This image is so generally accepted that men who do not fit these categories – men who are well-dressed, middle-class and polite to their elders – are simply not plausible rapists. When women are attacked by these men their experiences will, in general, be categorized as sex rather than rape – hence the difficulties women have in establishing non-consent in statistically typical rape cases.

Even if they are convicted of rape, men who do not qualify as monsters will not experience the full weight of the law. A particularly chilling example of this was provided by the English Court of Appeal when it reduced from three years to six months the sentence of a soldier convicted of raping a 17-year-old girl. As well as raping her the man had pulled his victim's earrings out, thrust his ringed hand up her vagina, and left her with the kind of swelling usually only caused by childbirth. Mr Justice Slynn stated that he was 'not ... a criminal in the sense in which that word is used frequently in these courts. Clearly he is a man who, on the night in question, allowed his enthusiasm for sex to overcome his normal behaviour.'

WOMEN PROVOKE RAPE

The idea that women provoke rape seems, at first glance, to be inconsistent with the notion that rapists are monsters. But the two operate in tandem. If a woman is seen as provocative, her attacker's actions can be explained as involuntary, uncontrolled reactions to her provocation. The attacker, then, is not a monster but is a normal man overcome by the lust inspired by his victim. Being a normal man, he is not a rapist and should not be convicted of rape.

RAPE BY AN ACQUAINTANCE IS NOT SO BAD

When a man was recently convicted of raping a woman with whom he had dinner, British Judge Prosser remarked: 'This is not in my view the more serious type of rape– that is the rape of a total stranger.' The same Judge Prosser had, six months previously, declined to imprison a 15-year-old who had been convicted of rape, instead ordering the boy to pay his victim £500 compensaion so that she could have a 'good holiday'.

Not all judges articulate their thinking quite so explicitly as Judge Prosser, but the sentencing guidelines laid down by the higher courts actually indicate that the sentence passed should be lower where the woman and her attacker have had a sexual relationship prior to the attack. The notion that rape by a non-stranger is less serious than rape by a total stranger is completely without foundation. It depends on the idea that rape is wrong because it is an attack on a woman as property, because it reduces the value of an otherwise pure, marketable commodity. This idea also lies behind the difficulties which sexually active women face in having their attackers convicted. If the woman is so soiled already, what difference does one more act of sexual intercourse make?

Judges who espouse these views might care to read the words of one woman who had herself been 'dragged off a London street and raped by strangers'. In a letter to the *Guardian* she wrote: 'I am now extremely careful as to where I go and when I go. This is distressing, but it might be more distressing had I been raped by someone that I knew and trusted, possibly in my own home ... Living in fear of male friends and relatives, male acquaintances, workmates and the plumber is no better than fearing strangers in dark alleyways. Dark alleyways are easier to avoid.'

RAPE IS A NON-VIOLENT CRIME

There is a widespread assumption amongst lawyers that rape isn't violent *in itself* – that the offence is only violent if additional force is used or threatened over and above that necessary to achieve unwanted penetration. Recently, for example, a Canadian judge ruled that the threat that: 'I am going to fuck you even if I have to rape you' did not amount to a threat of bodily harm, but an adoring fantasy.[42] And in 1992 in New York, Judge Nicholas Figueroa accepted that a man who had pinned a woman against a bathroom wall and sodomized her was not guilty of violence. The woman was 23 years old but had an IQ of 51, and the social functioning of a child. The judge also accepted that, because the woman had been raped before, the trauma of the attack would not have been so great.[43]

The notion that a second, third or tenth rape will be less traumatic than the first one depends on the view of rape as sex. If rape is sex, then rape won't really be a problem unless the woman is a virgin – she may be entitled to complain of technical violation otherwise, but no great harm is done unless she receives visible injuries.

If rape is less traumatic for the sexually experienced how much less traumatic again it must be for a prostitute. Her only complaint, it seems, is that she had taken from her something which she more usually sold. So, in 1992, the Supreme Court of Victoria, Australia, ruled that the rape of a prostitute was 'not as heinous as when committed on a happily married woman'. Being raped did not cause a prostitute 'a reaction of revulsion which it might cause in a chaste woman' because, according to the learned judges, 'prostitutes suffer little or no sense of shame or defilement when raped'. This prostitute testified that 'it was a time of degradation, complete degradation'.

PART 3

Conclusion

The Reality of Rape

I have looked at the way in which rape has been dealt with throughout history, and the way it is handled by the legal system. I have also considered some of the commonly held attitudes towards rape. The overwhelming message is that only some rapes are taken seriously, only some rapists are punished. The rapes which are taken seriously are rapes by strangers; rapes which happen to 'good' women; rapes which result in serious visible injury. Now it is time to see how this picture of rape (which of course excludes date rape), fits with the reality of rape as it actually happens.

HOW OFTEN DOES RAPE HAPPEN?

You could be forgiven for asking why there is so much fuss about rape at all, since the crime occupies a very small position in the statistics. Even though reported rapes (and attempted rapes) have increased to a staggering extent in recent years (from 240 in England

and Wales in 1947 to 1338 in London alone in 1993), still, in the UK in 1993, all sexual offences accounted for less than 1 per cent of recorded crimes. The statistics indicate that the chance of being raped in any one year is measured as one in thousands (in 1991, for example, one in 7539). Over a lifetime, this translates into chances of being raped that are well under one in a hundred. So, it could be argued that women's fear of rape is wildly out of proportion to the dangers which we actually face.

This would be true if the official statistics actually told us how common rape is. But they come nowhere near painting an accurate picture. All the many surveys that have been carried out, both here and in the US, show that rape is vastly more common than the official figures show. In London in 1982, for example, a study carried out by Women Against Rape found that one woman in every six had been raped, and that a further one in five had suffered an attempted rape. One in seven married women had been raped by their husbands. Of the women raped by other men, fewer than one in ten had reported the crime to the police.[1]

In the United States, surveys have consistently come up with even higher figures for rape. Diane Russell's 1978 survey of women in San Francisco indicated that one in four had been raped, and that three in ten had suffered an attempted rape – the total proportion of women who had suffered rape and/or attempted rape was a staggering 44 per cent.[2] And Dean Kilpatrick's survey, carried out a few years later, also showed a one-in-four rape rate.[3]

These and many other surveys showed that rape was much more common than had previously been thought. They also showed that rapists were not the mad strangers of the popular imagination – most attackers were known to their victims, and many of them were dating. Despite the general consistency in findings across the various surveys, some have been widely criticized. The fact that many women defined as raped by the researchers had not applied that term themselves, has caused many to suggest that these women were not in fact raped. But if a woman has answered 'yes' to the question 'Have you ever had vaginal sex with a man because he threatened you with physical injury?', then the woman is reporting rape whether she knows it or not.

It is often suggested that these surveys included as rape sex which was secured by 'verbal coercion'. This caused many wags to remark that 'old-fashioned persuasion' is enough now to get a man accused of rape. But this is entirely untrue. Mary Koss and her colleagues (who were among the most heavily criticised) did ask women about 'sexual coercion' ('sexual intercourse obtained through the aggressor's misuse of authority, or his continual arguments or pressure') and 'unwanted sexual contact' (fondling, kissing, petting and so on, either as a result of verbal coercion, misuse of authority or the use of force or threats). But these figures were tallied separately from those for rape or attempted rape. If they were added to the 27.5 per cent of rape or attempted rape, the total proportion of women who had been sexually victimized in some way by the time they were 21 was a staggering 53.7 per cent.[4]

WHO GETS RAPED?

Young girls are much more likely to be raped than older women. Sixty-one per cent of the rapes reported to the massive 1992 study *Rape in America* had happened when the women were less than 18 years old, and almost 30 per cent when they were children younger than 12.[5] US Department of Justice statistics tell a similar story: although the under-18s account for only 25 per cent of the female population, they suffered over half of the rapes recorded by the police in 1994.[6] Some victims of rape are incredibly young – in England in 1994 a father was jailed for raping his 13-month-old baby.

Children suffering from developmental disabilities are between four and ten times more likely to be sexually assaulted than are non-disabled children. And the vulnerability doesn't stop when they grow up; US statistics suggest that 90 to 100 per cent of disabled women will be sexually assaulted as many as four times in their lives.[7]

Studies carried out both in the UK and the US show that many women raped as adults had also been physically or sexually abused as children or adolescents. A 1994 Oxford study found that half of all those who were sexually abused in college had been abused previously.[8] This was similar to the childhood/adolescent victimization rates of the adult women who reported rape and attempted rape to Diane Russell in San Francisco in 1978. And *Rape in America* records that almost half of these women who reported rape had experienced it more than once; 5 per cent had been raped so many times they had lost count. A psychologist involved in treating victims of sexual assault suggests: 'It's just like wildlife films ... Perpetrators look for the weak, those unable to defend themselves, those who can be separated from the herd ... There's a system of predator and prey ... I see two-month old babies victimized, and they are part of the system. The only thing victims do wrong is that they are helpless or learn to be helpless.'[9]

Sexual abuse, particularly when it happens to children, teaches the victim that she can't control what happens to her body – it teaches her that resistance is futile. And so she is easier to abuse the second time around. Because the young victim lacks the ability correctly to interpret what is happening when she is sexually abused, she is more likely to blame herself for what has happened, and to 'feel powerless to thwart others who try to harm her in the future'.[10]

Men who force sex on women and girls abuse their victims' minds as well as their bodies. Small wonder, then, that many women who are raped by men they know (42 per cent according to Koss) have sexual contact with their attackers afterwards. This finding, which Koss regarded as 'among the most disturbing' she made has been taken by many to mean that they *couldn't* have been raped.[11] Fairly typical was the remark of one man, writing in the *Guardian* that 'women who are raped are not generally known for going back for more sex with their assailants'.[12] Robin Warshaw suggests that women 'went back for more' because they didn't recognize what had happened to them as rape. Because they interpreted rape according to the stereotypes, they didn't define straightforward forced sex with someone they knew, particularly someone they were dating, as rape. One stated: 'I thought that he truly did care for me and I blamed myself for what happened … I … felt like I was such a tramp, that it was my fault.

Sometimes, Warshaw explains, the raped woman 'sees the man who raped her again in order to turn the rape into an experience of sexual intercourse that happened in the context of an ongoing relationship and, therefore, to make it acceptable.'[13] And what happened to the women who slept with their rapists again? Usually they got raped again – the average raped woman was raped twice by the same man.

Women aren't just made vulnerable by youth, disability and previous assault. In 1990, the *Guardian* reported the results of an enormous investigation into rape and sexual harassment in the US armed forces; 38 per cent of the women had experienced physical sexual harassment in the armed forces, and 5 per cent had been raped. These women were active servicewomen trained in combat.[14] But they worked in an environment which is overwhelmingly male, and one in which, it seems, they had learned not to expect complaints of sexual harassment or assault to be taken seriously. This made them vulnerable.

Finally, the very fact that rape is seen as a matter of shame in most societies increases women's exposure to it. In 1991 the *Independent* reported Amnesty International's chilling claim that women 'are often raped in custody'.[15] Amnesty accused state security agents in more than forty nations of 'barbaric' treatment of women prisoners. 'Rape is sometimes the torture method of choice simply because the social stigma in many cultures virtually guarantees that women won't talk about it afterwards.'

Such use of rape is not new. During the Second World War Japanese troops raped Chinese women. The Germans raped Belgian women and the Russians raped Germans. The Japanese authorities sanctioned the kidnap of hundreds of thousands of Korean, Chinese, Taiwanese, Philippina and other women who were held as 'comfort women' for Japanese troops. These women were raped tens of times each day, as well as being starved and tortured. Only 25 per cent of the women survived their captivity.[16] US soldiers, too, raped and murdered countless women in Vietnam, and Pakistani troops raped Bangladeshi women in 1971. Iraqi troops raped Kuwaiti women during the occupation, and in June 1993 the *Guardian* reported that torture and rape by Indian forces in Kashmir were widespread. In November 1993, the *Guardian* stated that the 'everpresent threat' of rape for Somali women living in Kenyan refugee camps was driving the women back home. It also reported Amnesty's allegations that women and girls as young as 14 were frequently gang-raped by Indonesian forces in custody and field operations.[17]

Rape in wartime serves not only to humble the defeated – it can also help to settle the future of disputed territory. By spring 1993, for example, it was estimated that between 20,000 and 50,000 Muslim women had been raped by Serbian forces in the former Yugoslavia. Many of these women had been repeatedly assaulted, impregnated, and then detained until it was too late for them to seek abortions.

WHO REALLY RAPES?

Who do we think of when we think of rape? The stranger – the man who jumps from the alleyway as we walk home at night, the terrifying intruder who waits for our return. We allow our lives to be constricted, our horizons narrowed by the terror of rape. So who should we really fear?

Diane Scully's study of convicted rapists found that men who rape are normal: they are not ill or sexually deprived. They are almost indistinguishable from other men. Comparing the rapists with other convicts, Scully found that three quarters of all convicts thought that a man should not give up when a woman refused sex. The only significant differences between rapists and non-rapists were that the rapists were more inclined to put some women on pedestals and to regard other women as deserving what happened if they were raped. In addition, slightly more rapist than non-rapist men believed that men were justified in using physical violence on women, and that some women liked to be hit.[18]

Scully's findings echoed those of others that men who raped were 'otherwise ordinary guys who think it's OK to control and dominate women'. Almost 30 per cent of the women who reported rape to Women Against Rape's 1985 London survey had been raped by their husbands; and a further 54 per cent of the women knew their attackers. A 1994 Oxford study found that 89 per cent of those raped were attacked by people they knew.[19]

WHY DO MEN RAPE?

Diane Scully's study of imprisoned rapists suggests that, contrary to popular belief, sexual frustration or arousal have very little to do with rape. Men did not generally rape because they were driven by 'irrational, subconscious and uncontrollable' motivations. The decision to rape was, instead, usually 'overt and deliberate'.[20] In this, Scully's findings coincided with the views of Carol Sellars, a psychologist at Broadmoor, one of England's high-security hospitals: 'If you actually talk to rapists, in most cases it's about two things. One is about asserting domination and humiliating the victim, and sexual degradation is seen as the ultimate form of degradation. The other is to do with asserting masculinity, which again is essentially about domination and aggression.'[21]

Rape is, it seems, a form of punishment, and men give themselves licence to rape women of whose behaviour they do not approve. Seventeen per cent of Scully's rapists excused their own behaviour on the grounds that their victims had worn 'seductive' clothes. Scully also found 'that some men will not call the offence rape if the victim violates traditional standards of female behaviour by, for example, being alone in a bar or accepting a lift from someone met casually.'[22] Nor is this type of attitude confined to the kind of rapist who ends up in prison. One study of self-disclosed acquaintance rapists, for example, found that two-thirds of them, while accepting legal guilt, considered that their victims' behaviour entirely absolved them from blame. Many of these men had been involved in gang-rape.[23] Women's behaviour and appearance do, it seems, contribute to rape. But they contribute not by causing a loss of self-control, as is commonly supposed, but by marking them out to their attackers as women whom it's OK to rape.

HOW DOES RAPE HAPPEN?

The popular picture of rape involves a woman beaten into submission or confronted with a lethal weapon such as a gun or a knife. Some men who rape do use weapons against their victims. Some choose to inflict injury over and above what is necessary in order to accomplish the act of rape itself. Many more simply use their superior size and strength, together with the threat of their fists if necessary. Mary Koss, for example, found that many acquaintance rapes 'are accomplished by the man simply using the weight of his body to hold the woman down'.[24] The violence often consists in the rape itself (together with any explicit or implied threats) – unwanted penetration is just as real an assault as a punch in the mouth. And Koss's findings in this respect are consistent with those of Finkelhor and Yllo, who studied wife rape.[25] They found that the difference between raping husbands who used additional violence against their wives and raping husbands who did not was one of weight – the more violent men were almost two stone lighter.

Rape in America reported that over 70 per cent of women who were raped sustained no physical injury at all. Of the remaining women, the vast majority received only minor physical injuries – only 4 per cent of women were left with serious physical injury.[26] The lack of physical injury might be taken to suggest that rape is, at its least serious, little more than a minor trespass by one person on the body of another. This is certainly the impression that we are frequently given by those who talk of acquaintance and, more particularly, date rape as non-violent rape, friendly rape, felonious gallantry, assault with failure to please.[27] But half the women surveyed by *Rape in America* feared serious injury or death at the time when they were being raped. The others were frozen with fright, and many dissociated or blacked out because of the shock of the attack. Because acquaintance, and particularly date rapes can happen very quickly, the victim is often too late to prevent the assault by the time she realizes what is happening.

Whether a woman struggles or not, rape can never be a simple, non-violent taking of sex – in order to secure the sexual contact the women must be overpowered, whether by fear, injury or by the simple application of superior strength. Linda Fairstein, New York's chief sex-crime prosecutor, stated recently that 'In twenty years of prosecuting sex offenses, I have never had a case in which the only expression of lack of consent was the victim's verbalization of the word "no", without any display of force or threats by the aggressor.'[28] Rape is a crime of violence.

Rape in America found (in contrast with the general absence of visible injuries), that raped women often suffered 'profound' psychological injuries as a result of rape. Around a third of the women reported major depression; the same proportion reported post traumatic stress disorder and the same proportion had contemplated suicide; 13 per cent attempted it. Rape victims, the study found, were three times more likely to have experienced depression than those who had not been raped, four times more likely to have contemplated suicide and thirteen times more likely to have made an attempt. They also showed substantially heavier use of alcohol and of illegal drugs, and were 13 and 26 times respectively more likely to have serious alcohol and drug problems. In the majority of cases, their alcohol or other drug use had started after they had been raped.[29]

Unfortunately, women who display these kinds of symptoms are less likely to be believed as rape victims than those who do not. At the same time, however, failure to show some culturally acceptable symptoms of 'rape trauma syndrome' will, it seems, raise the presumption that sex was consented to.[30] Raped women, it seems, just can't win.

It is frequently assumed that non-stranger rapes are less traumatic for their victims than are rapes committed by strangers. But research shows that there is little difference in the psychological injury suffered by the victims of stranger and acquaintance rape.[31] To the extent that any difference does exist, there is some suggestion that acquaintance rape leaves deeper scars. At least one study has found that 'Acquaintance-rape victims rate themselves less recovered than do stranger-rape victims for up to three years following their rape experiences.'[32] Women raped by acquaintances are less likely to seek counselling, and more inclined to repress their feelings about their assaults.[33] Yet another study suggested that the victims of acquaintance rape suffered more from self and societal blame for their failure to prevent the assault.[34]

WOMEN'S LIES ABOUT RAPE

We are by now very familiar with the assumption that women often lie about having been raped. Let's look at the true picture. Women do, very occasionally, make false allegations of rape. In April 1993, for example, a woman was convicted of wasting police time after she faked her own kidnapping and later claimed that she had been raped. She was suffering from bulimia nervosa and had acted in order to avoid the Christmas festivities.[35] In March 1994, *The Times* reported that a woman had been jailed for 28 days when she admitted wasting police time. She had had sex with a stranger and then claimed to have been raped.

These do happen; but numbers of false allegations is infinitesimal, and appears significant only because each incident is pounced upon with unwholesome relish by those who would have us believe in the myth of the vindictive accuser. On the strength of a couple of cases and some apocryphal stories the media give the impression that men are under constant threat of false allegation by vindictive or inadequate women. All the evidence shows that false claims of rape are very uncommon, and that claims against particular men (as opposed to vague stories about assault by unidentified strangers) are even more unusual.

The real lies that are told about rape are told by women who pretend that they have not been raped when, in fact, they have. In 1983 the British Crime Survey estimated that 74 per cent of sexual assaults in England and Wales went unreported. The following year they estimated the unreported Scottish figure at 93 per cent. The real figure of unreported rapes is probably much higher. We have already seen that many women who are raped according to the legal definition fail to define their experiences as rape because they know their attacker, or blame themselves for sex forced upon them.

Unofficial studies are rather better at discovering the extent of under-reporting; they tend to use same-sex interviews, avoid using the word 'rape' (asking instead about whether women were 'physically forced' to have sex), and to lead into questions about sexual assaults so as to give women permission to admit that they have been sexually victimized.[36]

These surveys not only indicate the extent of under-reporting, but can also indicate the types of rape which are least likely to be reported and the reasons why women fail to report. There is no guarantee, of course, that any survey will pick up on all rapes and other sexual assaults but special, targeted surveys do tend to make a better job of it than more general studies. The picture which emerges is this. No more than 10 per cent of the sexual assaults which take place in the UK, the US, Canada (and, as far as we know, anywhere else) are reported to the police[37] and those which are least likely to be reported are those committed by men known to their victims. Diane Russell, for example, found that less than 7 per cent of rapes committed by the victims' friends or dates were reported, in comparison with 30 per cent of stranger rapes. Failure to report was generally the result of women's fear that the police would be unhelpful and unsympathetic.[38] Similarly in 1990, women soldiers in the US consistently failed to report sexual harassment ranging from catcalls to rape; women were deterred from reporting by their fear of reprisals, and by their belief that their complaints would not be taken seriously. Men were more than twice as likely to complain of assaults as were women.

Even when women have been systematically tortured and raped, they are ashamed. The 'comfort women' who were incarcerated in military brothels by the Japanese authorities during the Second World War were shunned on their return to their homes. According to one woman: 'My adopted family and villagers called me dirty and didn't want to have me around'; and another: 'I have lived a life of shunning people out of fear of revealing my disgraceful past. I decided not to marry because I was so ashamed of my past.'[39]

Women who know their rapists are even more likely to feel shame. They often feel that they are partly to blame for the attack: they should have known what was going to happen; they should not have trusted the man; they should not have allowed themselves to be alone with their attacker; they must somehow have led the man on, given him the wrong impression. A woman who had been raped on holiday by a man who had tricked her into his apartment before using threats and physical force to overcome her resistance 'wondered whether she "qualified" for rape crisis services because her assailant was "obviously not a criminal or a rapist". She worried that she was responsible for misleading her attacker by agreeing to go with him to his apartment'. In this she had a lot in common with many other women raped by men they know – the victims of acquaintance rape, as well as those who were drinking or taking drugs when the rape happened, 'are less likely to feel entitled to care and assistance from medical and legal agencies.'[40]

Would it make things worse if the women defined themselves as raped? Commentators such as Kate Roiphe suggest that, in naming their experiences as rape, women embrace their status as victim, disempower themselves, perhaps create as a trauma what might otherwise go unnoticed. If this is true, it might be a better thing to overlook rapes which were not recognized as such by their victims. Women's speedy and complete recovery is, after all, more important than punishment and retribution. But it is clear that the damage done by rape is not confined to women who are able to attach the correct legal name to their experience. Koss's study found that, whether or not raped women defined themselves as such, 30 per cent contemplated suicide after the attack, 31 per cent sought psychotherapy and 82 per cent said that they had been forever changed by the experience.[41]

Why does it hurt so much? Is the damage that rape does, as those like Roiphe suggest, an archaic relic of our value as women having been defined in relation to our purity? Would the hurt stop if we accepted that we are people, and should be valued for ourselves and our actions rather than the extent to which our sexual organs are unused? This argument is attractive. But it depends upon the assumption that rape is a simple taking of sex without permission, that rape hurts women only because we think that it renders unpure something we wish to keep in reserve for another man. If this were the case, it would only require that we realize that rape is not our fault (and that, therefore, we are 'unsullied' by it), in order for the pain to go away. But women don't experience rape as a simple unauthorized taking of sex. You don't need to be a virgin to feel violated by rape. Because the essence of the violation that is rape is not sexual contact itself, but the fact that this contact takes place against our will. It is this that makes rape humiliating, degrading, devaluing. It's not our sexual organs that are being devalued, it's our human status, our right to control our own bodies, our sexual freedom.

PUTTING RAPE IN CONTEXT

Rape doesn't stand on its own as a crime that men commit against women. Instead, it forms one part of an entire spectrum of violence that women experience at the hands of men. The violence ranges from verbal sexual harassment at work and on the street to murderous assaults, usually by current or ex-husbands or lovers. Many scorn the suggestion of a link between rape and sexual harassment. But the point is an important one. Sexual harassment, whether it takes place on the street or in the workplace, is men's way of telling us that we are in their space. We have ventured onto their territory, and we are there on their sufferance. This becomes apparent as soon as a woman reacts in a hostile way to a catcall or a wolf-whistle: what started off as 'hello luv', 'give us a smile' is very quickly translated into expressions of fury, and the fury is almost invariably directed against the women as woman. She isn't a 'rude bastard' – she is a 'cunt', a 'fat slag', an 'ugly bitch'.

The general casualness with which sexual harassment is treated teaches us that we need not expect our rapes to be taken seriously either. Harassment creates a hostile environment; the US servicewomen who did not report that they had been raped by their colleagues learnt not to do so, presumably, because of the manner in which complaints of sexual harassment had been handled.

As for physical violence against women, it begins terrifyingly early. In 1994 an American study found that a third of adolescents had experienced physical abuse in a dating relationship, and one quarter had suffered sexual violence. The report's conclusion is terrifying: 'Relationship problems usually surface after age 14, when young men develop the upper body strength that can be used to dominate young women.'[42] Problems of violence against women, it seems, start just as early as men are big enough to overpower us.

And the problems get worse over time. More than 50 per cent of the women and children who were homeless in the US in 1994 were fleeing male violence. The few cases which are prosecuted tend to come to little. In England, in 1990, Helena Kennedy QC wrote: 'Wife battering tends to be subject to a lower charge, such as common assault, even in cases where injuries amount to actual bodily harm. This means that the cases are often assigned to magistrates' courts and are treated less seriously than other types of assault. In the few cases where they do go for trial, acquittal rates are high and fines are the most common punishment. Imprisonment is the least frequent outcome (a mere 6 per cent in 1990 according to Home Office statistics).'[43]

One London survey, carried out in 1993, found that 'nearly two out of three men admit they would use violence on their wives or partners in "conflict" situations'. If confronted with infidelity, being 'nagged', a partner arriving late home without explanation, a heated row, or when expectations over housework or childcare were not met, almost one man in five said he would react violently every time. And a similar number confessed to having resorted to violence in at least two of those situations. Almost one third of the women interviewed had been punched or slapped, kicked, headbutted, struck with a weapon or suffered attempted strangulation.[41] And these assaults are trivialized.

Even when men kill their partners, they are often treated leniently by the courts. In the UK, almost half of the women who are murdered are murdered by a current or former partner. Still they are excused on the basis that they were drunk, or because their wives nagged them. Sara Thornton was imprisoned for life for killing her alcoholic, abusing husband after he threatened to kill her. Two days after her appeal was rejected, Joseph McGrail received a two-year suspended sentence. He had kicked his wife to death as she lay drunk. The woman, declared Mr Justice Popplewell, 'would have tried the patience of a saint'.[45]

Some women are raped by strangers who jump on them from behind dark bushes at night. Some women are raped by strangers who break into their home. Many more women are raped by men who are not strangers to them. Women are raped by their husbands, they are raped by their boyfriends, they are raped by ex-partners and family friends. They are raped in the sanctity of their marriage bed, in the flats they share with their lovers, in the homes of their friends. These women are raped in the legal sense of that word – their bodies are penetrated without their consent, usually by men who know that they are unwilling, sometimes by men who simply couldn't care less. Most of these attacks, however, do not fit the cultural stereotype of rape. These women are left to pick up the pieces alone.

THE CASE FOR TAKING THE DATE OUT OF RAPE

References

CHAPTER 1 – DATE RAPE IN CONTEXT

1. The *Independent*, 21 March 1995.
2. The *Guardian*, 20 October 1993.
3. The *Sunday Telegraph*, 2 October 1994.
4. The *Guardian*, 25 January 1992.
5. See Adlers, Z. *Rape on Trial* (London: Routledge and Kegan Paul, 1987).
6. *The Times*, 20 October 1993.
7. *The Times*, 2 November 1993.
8. The *Guardian*, 9 March 1995.

CHAPTER 2 – A BRIEF HISTORY OF RAPE

1. The theory was that, if the woman had cried out, someone would have come to her rescue.
2. Attenborough, F. *The Laws of the Earliest English Kings* (Cambridge, Cambridge University Press, 1922) pp. 5–17.
3. Simpson, A. 'The blackmail myth and the prosecution of rape and its attempt in 18th-century London: the creation of a legal tradition' *Journal of Criminal Law and Criminology* (1986) vol. 77, p. 118.
4. Kaye, J. (ed.) *Hale M. Placita Corone* (London, Seldon Society, 1966) Supplementary Series 4, p. 629.
5. Mill, J. (ed.) 'The subjection of women' (1868) in Rossi, A. (ed) *Essays on Sex Equality* (Chicago, University of Chicago Press, 1970) p. 160.

6. G v G, cited in Scutt, J., 'Consent in rape: the problem of the marriage contract' *Monash University Law Review* vol. 3, p. 349.

7. *Tomkins* 111 A 599, p. 601, discussed in Biggs, F., 'Rape law in Massachusetts: our Puritan forebears and other cultural remnants' *New England Law Review* (1989) vol. 22, p. 115.

8. Morris & Turner, 'Two problems in the law of rape' (1952–55) 2 *University of Queensland Law Journal* 256, p. 259, discussed by Scutt, note 5 above.

9. Lord Lane C J, in *R v Steel* (1977) 65 *Criminal Appeal Reports* 65.

10. Post, J. 'Ravishment of women and the Statutes of Westminster' in Baker, J. (ed.) *Legal Records and the Historian* (London, Royal Historical Society, 1978).

11. See generally Toner, B. *The Facts of Rape* (London, Hutchinson & Co, 1977), pp. 96–8.

12. Post, note 9 above. p. 155.

13. Blackstone, W. *Commentaries on the Laws of England 1765–69* (Chicago, University of Chicago Press, 1979), 5th ed., p. 213.

14. *R v Nicholl*, Gloucester Assizes Summer 1807 in *Crown Cases Reserved* (1825), pp. 130–2.

15. Jones, D. *Crime in Nineteenth Century Wales* (Cardiff, University of Wales Press, 1992).

16. Dr Tait, *Diseases of Women and Abdominal Surgery* (Leicester, Richardson, 1889) p. 56, cited by Edwards, S. *Female Sexuality and the Law* (Oxford, Robertson, 1981), p. 126.

17. *State v Hartigan* 32 Vt 607, discussed in Block, M. *An Association Easily to be Made: A History of Rape Law in Nineteenth-Century State Appellate Courts 1800–1870* (University of Louisville, 1992), M.A. Thesis, pp. 105–7.

18. 1 Fla 298 (1847), discussed in Wriggins, J. 'Rape, racism and the law' *Harvard Women's Law Journal* (1983) vol. 6, p. 103.

19. 37 Miss 316 discussed in Marsh, J. Geist, A. and Caplan, N. *Rape and the Limits of Law Reform* (Boston Massachusetts, Auburn House Publishing Co, 1982), p. 102.

20. Bienen & Field, cited by Biggs, note 6 above, p. 94.

21. Kilpatrick, D. et al, *Rape in America: A Report to the Nation* (Medical University of South Carolina, National Victim Centre and Crime Victims Research and Treatment Centre, 1992), p. 4.

22. Carter, J. *Rape in Medieval England* (University Press of America, 1985).

23. Clark, A. *Women's Silence, Men's Violence: Sexual Assault in England, 1770–1845* (London, Pandora, 1987), p. 24.

24. *State v Ellison* 19 NM 428, pp. 437–8 and *Anderson v State* 82 Miss 784. p. 788, both cited in Remick, L. Read her lips *University of Pennsylvania Law Review* (1993) vol. 141, p. 1103.

25. Carter, note 21 above.

26. Post, note 9 above.

27. Kaye, note 3 above.

28. Post, note 9 above.

29. Ruggeiero, G. *The Boundaries of Eros: Sex Crime and Sexuality in Renaissance Venice* (Oxford, Oxford University Press, 1985), chapter V.

THE CASE FOR TAKING THE DATE OUT OF RAPE

30. Radzinowicz, L. *History of English Criminal Law* (London, Stevens, 1948–68), pp. 148 and 155.
31. Beattie, J. *Crime and the Courts in England 1660–1800* (Princeton New Jersey, Princeton University Press, 1986); McLynn, F. *Crime and Punishment in Eighteenth Century England* (London, Routledge, 1989).
32. See generally Toner, note 10 above, chapter 5.
33. Clarke, note 22 above, pp. 65–6.
34. McLynn, note 30 above.
35. *The Times*, 25 October 1825.

CHAPTER 3 – THE BIRTH OF DATE RAPE

1. The *Guardian*, 20 October 1993.
2. The *Guardian*, 21 October 1993.
3. The *Guardian*, 29 October 1993.
4. The *Daily Mirror*, 24 November 1994.
5. The *Guardian*, 8 December 1994.
6. 24 November 1994.
7. *The Times*, 28 May 1994.
8. *Independent on Sunday* 19 June 1994.
9. *Sunday Telegraph*, 2 October 1994.
10. *Observer*, 25 November 1990.
11. The *Guardian*, 28 November 1990.
12. Russell, D. *Rape in Marriage*, (New York, Macmillan, 1982).
13. The *Guardian*, 28 November 1990.
14. Connell, N. and Wilson, C. (eds.), *Rape: The First Sourcebook for Women* (New York, New American Library, 1974).
15. See generally Estrich, S. *Real Rape* (Cambridge Massachusetts, Harvard University Press, 1987).
16. MacDonald, J. *Rape Offenders and Their Victims* (Springfield, Thomas Books, 1971).
17. *New York Times*, 28 December 1990.
18. See Estrich, note 15 above, pp. 35–38.

CHAPTER 4 – THE FORCES OF DENIAL IN THE MEDIA

1. S. Gutmann, 'Date rape: does anyone really know what it is?' *Playboy*, October 1990. Cited in Ingram, J. 'Date rape: it's time for "no" to really mean "no"' *American Journal of Criminal Law* (1993) vol. 21(1), p. 3, at p. 9.
2. (London, Weidenfield & Nicholson, 1993), pp. 177–8.
3. Thomas, note 2 above.
4. The *Guardian*, 29 October 1993.
5. Brown, K. 'The social construction of a rape victim: stories of African-American males about the rape of Desiree Washington' *University of Illinois Law Review* (1992), p. 997, at p. 1005.
6. The *Guardian*, 20 October 1993.
7. Thomas, note 2 above, p. 179.

8.   Roiphe, K. *The Morning After Sex: Fear, and Feminism on Campus* (Boston, Little, Brown, 1993), p. 80. The MacKinnon quotation is taken (out of context) from MacKinnon, C. *Feminism Unmodified: Discourses on Life and Law* (Cambridge Massachusetts, Harvard University Press, 1987), p. 82.

9.   *Chatelaine*, July 1994.

10.   27 November 1994.

11.   Russell, D. *Rape in Marriage* (New York, Macmillan, 1982).

12.   Finkelhor, D. and Yllo, K. *License to Rape* (New York, Rinehart & Winston, 1985) p. 114.

13.   Thomas, note 2 above, pp. 182–3.

14.   *Los Angeles Times*, 30 October 1994.

15.   *San Diego Union Tribune*, 26 August 1994.

16.   Note 12, above, p. 18.

17.   26 March 1995.

18.   The programme was broadcast in early 1994.

19.   19 June 1994.

20.   27 October 1993.

21.   Note 2, above, p. 186.

22.   17 December 1994.

23.   See the *Guardian* 2 May 1991 for comment.

CHAPTER 5 – THE FORCES OF DENIAL IN SOCIETY

1.   20 March 1994.

2.   The *Guardian*, 11 November 1993.

3.   *Independent on Sunday Magazine*, 26 August 1990.

4.   *Story v State* 178 Ala 98, p. 104, discussed in Wriggins, J. 'Rape, racism and the law' *Harvard Women's Law Journal* (1983) vol.6, p. 103, at p. 127.

5.   Wriggins, note 4 above, p. 124; La Free. G. Reskin, B. and Vischer, C. 'Jurors' responses to victims' behaviour and legal issues in sexual assault trials' *Social Problems* (1985) vol. 32(4), p. 389.

6.   The *Independent*, 11 January 1991.

7.   31 January 1995.

8.   Burt, M. 'Cultural myths and supports for rape' *Journal of Personality and Social Psychology* (1980) vol. 38, p. 217, at p. 217.

9.   Barnett, N. and Field, H. 'Sex differences in university students' attitudes towards rape' *JC Student Personnel*, (1977) discussed in Friedland, S. 'Date rape and the culture of acceptance' *Florida Law Review* (1991) vol. 43, p. 487. See also Torrey, M. 'When will we be believed? rape myths and the idea of a fair trial in rape prosecutions' *University of California, Davis Law Review* (1991) vol. 24, p. 1013, at pp. 1039 ff.

10.   20 October 1993.

11.   Torrey, note 9 above, p. 1051.

12.   MacDonald, J. *Rape Offenders and Their Victims* (Springfield, Thomas Books, 1971).

13.   Elliott, D. 'Rape complainants' sexual experience with third parties' [1984] *Criminal Law Review*, p. 4, at pp. 13–14.

14. The *Guardian*, 6 February 1990.

15. The *Guardian*, 15 December 1989.

16. The distinction between 'justification' and 'excuse' follows Scully, D. and Marolla, J. 'Convicted rapists' vocabulary of motive: excuses and justifications' *Social Problems* (1984) vol. 31(5), p. 530 who distinguish between admitting and denying rapists who, respectively, excuse and justify their actions. See also Scully, D. *Understanding Sexual Violence: a Study of Convicted Rapists* (Boston, Unwin Hyman, 1990).

17. Field, H. and Bienen, L. *Jurors and Rape* (Lexington Massachusetts, Lexington Books, 1980), p. 55.

18. *St Louis Post-Dispatch*, 29 July 1994.

19. Malamuth, N. 'Rape proclivity among males' *Journal of Social Issues* (1981) vol. 37(4), p. 138; Murphy, W. Coleman, E. and Haynes, M. 'Factors related to coercive sexual behaviour in a nonclinical sample of males' *Violence and Victims* (1986) vol. 1, p. 255.

20. La Free, G. *Rape and Criminal Justice: The Social Construction of Sexual Assault* (Belmont California, Wadsworth, 1989), pp. 95–9.

21. *Correspondent*, 24 June 1990.

22. Delivering the Strathclyde and Glasgow Universities' Alexander Stone lecture in rhetoric (June 1991).

23. Deutsch, H. *The Psychology of Women* (1944) discussed by Edwards, S. *Female Sexuality and the Law* (Oxford, Robertson, 1981),pp. 103–105.

24. Kanin, E. 'Female rape fantasies: a victimisation study' *Victimology* (1982) vol. 7, p. 114, at p. 119: 'conscious fantasizing of rape by women as a sexually rewarding event appears to be something of a rare phenomenon'.

25. *Houston Chronicle*, 10 October 1992.

26. Abbey and Melby, 'The effects of nonverbal cues on gender differences in perceptions of sexual intent' *Sex Roles* (1986) vol. 15, p. 283, cited by Friedland, note 9 above, p. 489.

27. Johnson, C. Stockdale, M. and Saal, F. 'Persistence of men's misperceptions of friendly cues across a variety of interpersonal encounters' *Psychology of Women Quarterly* (1995) vol. 15, p. 463, at pp. 463 & 473.

28. J Kikuchi, 'Rhode Island develops successful intervention program for adolescents' *National Coalition Against Sexual Assault News*, Fall 1988 p. 26, cited by Torrey, note 9 above, p. 1021.

29. Scully, note 16, above, pp. 64 & 72.

30. Scully, note 16, above, p. 98.

31. The remaining 34 denied contact entirely so were excluded from study.

32. Kanin, E. 'Date rape: unofficial criminals and victims' *Victimology* (1984) vol. 9, p. 95.

CHAPTER 6 – THE FORCES OF DENIAL IN THE LEGAL SYSTEM

1. Sex with a sleeping woman is rape in England and Wales (a sleeping woman cannot consent) but not in Scotland (she will have no will).

2. S 213.1 Model Penal Code discussed in Finkelhor, D. & Yllo, K. *License to Rape* (New York, Rinehart & Winston, 1985), p. 149.

3. See generally Estrich, S. *Real Rape* (Cambridge Massachusetts, Harvard University Press, 1987).

4. 15 April 1991. Her name had been published in England by *The Sunday Mirror* (7 April). NBC followed suit (16 April), as did the *New York Times* (17 April).

5. *Star Tribune*, 20 December 1994.

6. National Institute of Law Enforcement and Criminal Justice, *Forcible Rape: A National Survey of Responses by Police* (US Dept of Justice, 1977).

7. Smith, L. *Concerns About Rape* (London HMSO, 1989), Home Office Research Studies 106.

8. Gregory, G. and Lees, S. *Rape and Sexual Assault: A Study of Attrition* (London, Islington Council, 1993).

9. Gregory and Lees, note 8 above.

10. The *Guardian*, 9 March 1995.

11. McCahill, T. Meyer, L. and Fischman, A. *The Aftermath of Rape* (Lexington Massachusetts, Lexington Books, 1979).

12. The *Guardian*, 2 November 1993.

13. Chambers, G. and Millar, A. *Investigating Sexual Assault* (Edinburgh, Scottish Office Central Research Unit, 1983).

14. Gregory and Lees, note 8 above.

15. Chambers and Millar, note 13 above.

16. Smith, note 7 above.

17. La Free, G. 'Official reactions to social problems: police decisions in sexual assault cases' *Social Problems* (1981) vol. 28(5), p. 582; Reskin, B. and Visher, C. 'The impact of evidence and extralegal factors in jurors' decisions' *Law and Society Review* (1986) vol. 20, p. 427; McCahill, Meyer & Fischman, note 11 above; Kerstetter, W. Gateway to justice *Journal of Criminal Law and Criminology* (1990) vol. 81, p. 267.

18. McCahill, Meyer & Fischman, note 11 above, pp. 105 & 241–2.

19. Marsh, J. Geist, A. and Caplan, N. *Rape and the Limits of Law Reform* (Boston Massachussetts, Auburn House Publishing Co, 1982) p. 93.

20. Gregory and Lees, note 8 above.

21. Adler, Z. *Rape on Trial* (London, Routledge & Kegan Paul, 1987), pp. 119–20.

22. Gregory and Lees, note 8 above, p. 55.

23. R v J SCCRM/91/452, discussed in Mack, K. 'Continuing Barriers to women's credibility' *Criminal Law Forum* vol. 4, p. 327 at pp. 348–9.

24. Edwards, S. *Female Sexuality and the Law* (Oxford, Robertson, 1981), pp. 127–8.

25. Schafran, L. 'Writing and reading about rape: a primer' *St John's Law Review* (1993) vol. 66, p. 979, at p. 1012; Adler, note 21 above, p. 25.

26. Catton, K. 'Evidence regarding the prior sexual history of an alleged rape victim – its effect on the perceived guilt of the accused' *University of Toronto Law Review* (1975) vol. 22, p. 165, at p. 173.

27. La Free, G. Reskin, B. and Vischer, C. 'Jurors' responses to victims' behaviour and legal issues in sexual assault trials' *Social Problems* (1985) vol. 32(4), p. 389, at p. 397.

28. Marsh, Geist and Caplan, note 19 above, pp. 177 ff & 133.

29. *Seaboyer*, 66 CCC (3d) 321.

30. *Redguard* [1991] Crim.L.R. 213.

31. *SMS* [1992] Crim.L.R. 310.

32. Estrich, note 3 above, p. 88 discussing Michigan's legislative provisions. See also Spohn, S. and Horney, J. *Rape Law Reform* (New York, Plenum Press, 1992), pp. 114ff.

33. See *Dispatches* (discussed in Chapter 4, p. 51), Andrews, K. 'The admissibility of other crimes evidence in acquaintance rape prosecutions' *Southern Illinois University Law Journal* (1993) vol. 17, p. 341.

34. Andrews, note 33 above, p. 357 discussing Brill, S. 'How the Willie Smith trial changed America' *American Lawyer* January/February 1992, p. 3.

35. Baroness Mallalieu (Labour peer, senior barrister and part-time judge) in the House of Lords.

36. Smith, J. *Mysogynies* (London, Faber and Faber, 1989), p. 3.

37. 31 October 1981, cited in Friedman L, *Crime and Punishment in American History* (New York, Basic Books, 1993), p. 216.

39. Sexual Offences Act 1956, s. 11.

40. *The Guardian*, 19 October 1993.

41. *The Guardian*, 3 July 1990.

42. *R v McGraw*, Ontario District Court 8 November 1988, discussed in Mahoney, K. *R v McGraw*: Rape fantasies v fear of sexual assault *Ottowa Law Review* vol. 21, p. 207.

43. Schafran, L. 'Maiming the Soul: judges, sentencing and the myth of the nonviolent rapist' *Fordham Urban Law Journal* (1993) vol. XX, p. 439.

CHAPTER 7 – CONCLUSIONS

1. Hall, R. *Ask Any Woman: London Inquiry into Rape and Sexual Assault* (Bristol, Falling Down Press, 1985).

2. Russell, D. *Sexual Exploitation: Rape, Child Abuse and Workplace Harassment* (Beverley Hills, California, Sage Publications, 1984).

3. Kilpatrick, D. et al. 'Criminal victimisation: lifetime prevalence, reporting to police, and psychological impact' *Crime and Delinquency* (1987) vol. 33, p. 479.

4. Koss, M. *et al.* 'The scope of rape: incidence and prevalence of sexual aggression and victimisation in a national sample of students in higher education' *Journal of Consulting and Clinical Psychology* (1987) vol. 55, p. 162; Warshaw, R. *I Never Called It Rape: The Ms Report on Recognizing, Fighting and Surviving Date and Acquaintance Rape* (New York, Harper & Row, 1988).

REFERENCES

5. Kilpatrick, D. *et al, Rape in America: A Report to the Nation* (Medical University of South Carolina, National Victim Centre and Crime Victims Research and Treatment Centre, 1992).

6. *St Louis Post Dispatch*, 9 July 1994. The paper's editorial notes that 'rapes are more likely to go unreported when the victim is young' and that '[t]he more circumscribed lives of girls mean that the perpetrators are more likely to be known to the victims. (Sceptics of date rape, take note)'.

7. *Phoenix Gazette*, 9 December 1994.

8. *The Guardian*, 20 December 1994.

9. *Plain Dealer*, 23 June 1994.

10. Gidycz et al. 'Sexual assault experience in adulthood and prior victimization experiences: a prospective analysis' *Psychology of Women Quarterly* (1993) vol. 17, p. 151.

11. Warshaw, note 4 above, p. 63.

12. *The Guardian*, 18 November 1993.

13. Warshaw, note 4 above, p. 63.

14. *The Guardian*, 13 September 1990.

15. 8 March 1991.

16. Parker, K. and Chew, J. 'Compensation for Japan's World War II war-rape victims' *Hastings International and Comparative Law Journal* (1994) vol. 17, p. 497, at pp. 498–9.

17. 10 November 1993.

18. Scully, D. *Understanding Sexual Violence: a Study of Convicted Rapists* (Boston, Unwin Hyman, 1990).

19. *The Guardian*, 20 December 1994.

20. *The Guardian*, 18 December 1990.

21. *The Guardian*, 20 January 1993.

22. *The Guardian*, 18 December 1990.

23. Kanin, E. 'Date rape: unofficial criminals and victims' *Victimology* (1984) vol. 9, p. 95, at p. 96–7.

24. Note 4, above, p. 61.

25. Finkelhor, D. and Yllo, K. *License to Rape* (New York, Rinehart & Winston, 1985).

26. Note 5, above. MacDonald, J. *Rape Offenders and Their Victims* (Springfield, Thomas Books, 1971) p. 93 discusses 1487 women sexually assaulted in the District of Columbia. 4.6 per cent suffered 'severe physical assault'. Only 18 were admitted into hospital. Six of these were children.

27. Bohmer, C. 'Judicial attitudes towards rape victims' in Chappell D. Geis R and Geis G (eds.), *Forcible Rape: The Crime, The Victim and the Offender* (New York, Columbia University Press, 1977), at p. 164.

28. Men, women and rape (panel discussion) *Fordham Law Review* (1994) vol. 64, p. 125, at p. 161.

29. Note 5 above, pp. 7–8.

30. Stefan, S. 'The protection racket: rape trauma syndrome, psychiatric labelling, and the law' *Northwestern University Law Review* (1994) vol. 88, p. 1271.

THE CASE FOR TAKING THE DATE OUT OF RAPE

31. Koss, M. Dinero, T. and Seible, C. 'Stranger and aquaintance rape: are there any differences in the victim's experience?' *Psychology of Women Quarterly* (1988) vol. 12, p. 1.

32. Katz, S. and Mazur, M. *Understanding the Rape Victim: a Synthesis of Research Findings* (New York, Wiley, 1979).

33. Warshaw, note 4 above.

34. Bowie, S. et al. 'Blitz rape and confidence rape: implications for clinical intervention' *American Journal of Psychotherapy* (1990) vol. 64, p. 180.

35. The *Guardian*, 8 April 1993.

36. For discussion of this see Koss, M. et al, 'The underdetection of rape: methodological choices influence incidence estimates' *Journal of Social Issues* (1992) vol. 48(1), p. 61.

37. Torrey, M. 'When will we be believed? rape myths and the idea of a fair trial in rape prosecutions' *University of California, Davis Law Review* (1991) vol. 24, p. 1013 at p. 1019 discussing G. Wyatt's study (reported in the *Los Angeles Times*, 17 October 1990).

38. Note 2, above. See also Russell, D. *Rape in Marriage* (New York, Macmillan, 1982); 'The prevalence and incidence of forcible rape and attempted rape of females' *Victimology* (1982) vol. 7, p. 81, *Sexual Exploitation: Rape, Child Abuse and Workplace Harassment* (Beverley Hills, California, Sage Publications, 1984), Wife rape, in Parrot, A. and Bechhofer, L. (eds), *Acquaintance Rape: The Hidden Crime* (New York, John Wiley & Sons, 1991).

39. Parker and Chew, note 16 above, p. 502.

40. Bowie *et al*, note 34 above, pp. 184–5.

41. Koss and Warshaw, note 4 above.

42. *St Louis Post Despatch*, 9 March 1994.

43. The *Independent*, 6 August 1990.

44. The *Independent* 18 January 1994, discussing Mooney J. *The Hidden Figure: Domestic Violence in North London* (London, Islington Council, 1994).

45. Birmingham Crown Court, 31 July 1991.